I-95
Bk.
U.S. RTE. 1
Freeport
Frost Gully
Allen Range Brook
UPPER MAST LANDING RD.
CEMETERY
Stream
Mill
Mast
anding
MAST LANDING
SANCTUARY
PLEASANT HILL ROAD
ROAD
Kelsey Brook
FLYING POINT
SCALE OF MILES
1/2
1/4
0
1 MILE
J. Luoma 83

N
BATH
I-95
BRUNSWICK
Freeport
TURNPIKE
PORTLAND
CASCO BAY
GULF of MAINE
MAINE
U.S. RTE 1
SACO

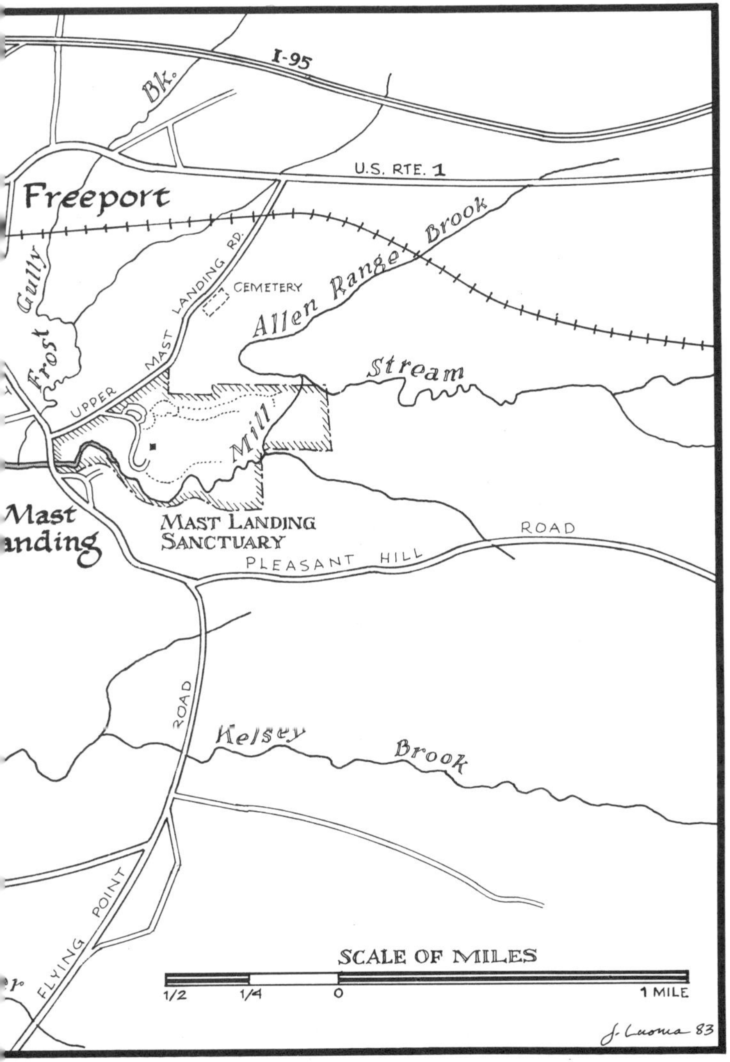

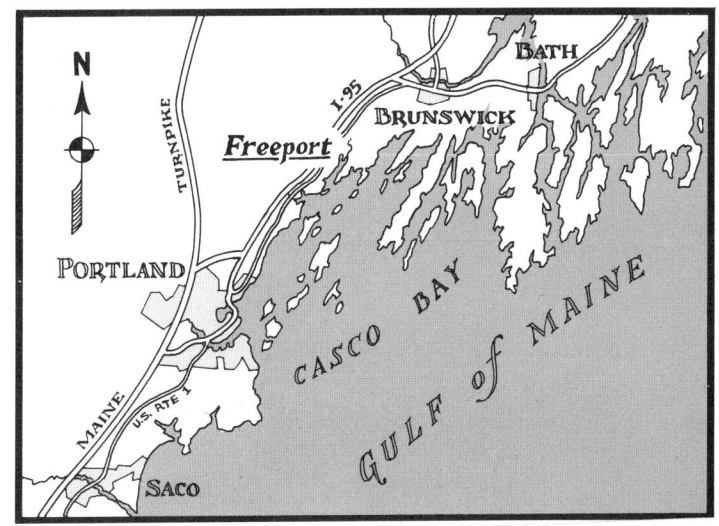

This publication was made possible
by a grant from the National
Endowment for the Humanities.

© Freeport Historical Society
Freeport, Maine 04032
1985

ISBN 0-9613259-0-9

TIDES *of* CHANGE

A GUIDE TO THE HARRASEEKET DISTRICT OF FREEPORT, MAINE

Text: Bruce Jacobson
          Joel W. Eastman
          Anne Bridges

Illustrations: Jon Luoma

ash splint basket

Contents

Preface

I. Introduction   1

II. Guide to The Harraseeket District

    1. Wolf Neck   9

    2. Mast Landing   23

    3. Porters Landing   37

    4. South Freeport   49

III. Conclusion   69

    Bibliography   77

Preface

This guide is about life in a part of Freeport, Maine known as the Harraseeket district which contains a remarkable record of coastal Maine when it was in its economic "Golden Age." The mid-nineteenth century was an age of material prosperity that was dependent on abundant local supplies of natural resources such as timber, fish, water-power, clay, salt hay, and granite. The guide is a sharing of what we have discovered through the Harraseeket Project about the ways that people utilized the natural resources of the Harraseeket watershed and how they affected, and in turn were affected by, the social and ecological systems that operated around them in the 1800s.

The guide includes information on both human and non-human inhabitants of the Harraseeket district. We have made every effort to present a factual image of the past and have only included information that we can support with contemporary, primary sources. The U.S. Census, newspapers, diaries, and other references provide statistics on the people who have lived on the shores of the Harraseeket estuary. Unfortunately, there has never been an inventory of the other life in the area.

We have a very incomplete picture of which plants and animals have lived on the shores and in the waters of the Harraseeket estuary. The lists of members of the biotic communities in each chapter should therefore be viewed with the following thoughts in mind. First, the boundaries between communities are indistinct and individuals often utilize several communities for feeding or other activities. Second, the number of individuals of a species, i.e. the species abundance, may change dramatically over time. For example, larval stages of mussels and clams are abundant in the water of the estuary during spring and early summer, and completely absent at other times; or, consider the numbers of minute animals that are very abundant in a rain puddle and then disappear entirely within a week of the rainstorm. Third, most people are not aware of the majority of the plants and animals that share our planet. As a result, the reader may be surprised to see the taxonomic group "chordates" — which includes people and most of the animals with which we are familiar — ranked very low in abundance compared to the other members of a biotic community.

It is our intent to offer glimpses of life in the district that illustrate the connections between all life. Times other than the 1800s have valuable lessons to teach about these connections. But, for now, we have chosen to focus on the rich record of the nineteenth century that survives in the Harraseeket district.

You are invited to become involved in learning about the connections between people and their environment in the Harraseeket district; first, through the text and activities in this guide and, later, by becoming involved in the programs of the Harraseeket Interpretive Project.

Bruce Jacobson, Director
Harraseeket Interpretive Project
February 1984

What is the Harraseeket Project?

The Harraseeket Interpretive Project conducts research and public programs which explore the interactions between people and the estuarine environment. Project activities are focused on the Harraseeket watershed in Freeport, Maine.

Programs have included:
1850s Coastal Life Program
  Explorations of saltwater farming and other activities in the 1850s for the general public.
Field Study Program - Field courses in "eco-history" for the general public.
Volunteer/Intern Program - Research and public programs conducted by volunteers and college students.
School Program - Classroom and field experiences for students K-12.

You are invited to become involved. For more information contact:
  Director
  Harraseeket Interpretive Project
  45 Main Street
  Freeport, Maine 04032

Part I - Introduction

The Guide

The story of change in the Harraseeket district forms a pattern common to many communities in Maine—early human use of coastal resources gave way to European settlement of the coast which, in turn, was followed by farming, shipbuilding, and industrialization. While the story is common, the Harraseeket district in Freeport is not.

The Harraseeket district includes the water of the Harraseeket River, the surrounding land, and all of the buildings located in four settlements associated with the river. The unique nature of the area was officially recognized in 1974 when the Harraseeket Historic District was placed on the National Register of Historic Places.

With the aid of this guide, one can retrace the steps in Freeport's evolution, not just in the pages of the book but in the remarkably unchanged landscape where it all happened. The land, water, and buildings that formed the backdrop for life in the town of Freeport during its first one hundred years can still be found today in the Harraseeket district. The following pages will guide the reader in exploring this fascinating area.

The chapters of the guide are each devoted to one of the geographic areas on the river settled in the 1800s: Wolf Neck, Mast Landing, Porters Landing, and South Freeport. The four chapters explore the socio-economic community that existed at each locale in the 1800s as well as one of the biotic communities—the water, mudflat, salt marsh or upland communities—located there. (All of the biotic communities existed at each of the settlements in the district; however, only one has been chosen to be highlighted at each locale.)

Knowledge of community members is key to understanding community life, so each chapter presents profiles of an individual person from the socio-economic community and a species of plant or animal from the biotic community. There are also lists of community members indicating the diversity of each community's inhabitants.

Finally, the guide is intended to be taken into the environment of the Harraseeket district. Activities and points of interest are included in each chapter to encourage the reader

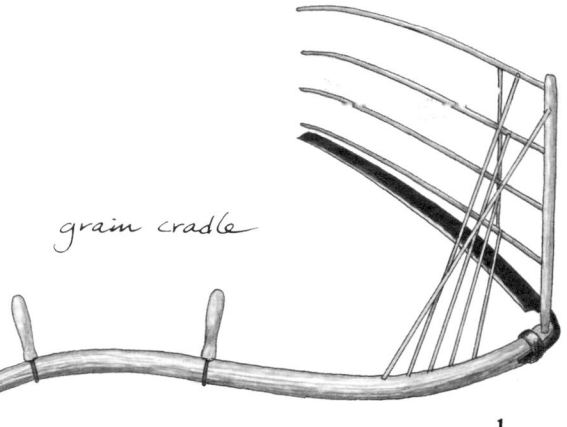
grain cradle

to take the guide in hand, walk the wooded trails, investigate the historic sites, visit a salt marsh, and see the places where the communities of the Harraseeket have been changing in relation to each other and the landscape for hundreds of years.

The Land

The land rises gradually from the shores of the Harraseeket River, reflecting the contours of the bedrock that lies beneath the soil and water. The bedrock forms a shallow basin with a gap in the southern rim, which allows ocean water to flow in and out forming the Harraseeket River.

All of the land that slopes down toward the river is called the Harraseeket watershed. Any rain or snow that falls there and is neither evaporated nor used by plants will flow via streams or drain through the soil and underlying bedrock into the Harraseeket.

Although there are three major watersheds in Freeport, the Harraseeket watershed is by far the largest, covering about 10,500 acres of land, a large part of all the land lying south and east of Interstate 95. The watershed is generally bordered by high land near Staples Point Road and Interstate 95 on the west, the Freeport-Brunswick town line on the north, and the Pleasant Hill and Wolf Neck roads on the east.

The Water

Although the Harraseeket is referred to as a river in conversation and on charts and maps, it is more accurately described as an estuary—an arm of the ocean where freshwater mixes with and dilutes the seawater that flows in freely with each high tide. The term estuary is also appropriate because, unlike most true freshwater rivers which flow downhill over many miles to the sea, the Harraseeket estuary is enclosed in a small basin and is affected by ocean tides throughout its entire course.

There are two high tides every day in the estuary, each one bringing 410 million cubic feet of ocean water into the Harraseeket, an amount of ocean water with every tide equal to the amount of water used in all of the homes in the state of Maine during a ten-day period. One result of this tremendous exchange of ocean water is that the Harraseeket flow reverses direction every six hours with the tide. The average height of the tide is about nine feet, although it can reach fourteen feet during the most extreme tides of the year.

Five major streams drain fresh water from the Harraseeket watershed into the estuary. The volume of fresh water entering the estuary in a six-hour period is equal to only about 0.2% of the amount of ocean water that enters the system every six hours. Therefore, the water in the Harraseeket is mixed, or brackish, water that is more like ocean water than fresh water in its chemical make-up.

The Buildings

Most of the buildings standing in the Harraseeket district today were built by Freeport residents in the 1800s to provide shelter for a growing

Pote house

population. The buildings created places for people to attend religious services, school, and social gatherings; to buy manufactured goods and imported food items; to build boats, saw lumber, grind grain, make shoes and barrels, and carry out other work of the day; to care for livestock and other farm animals; and, of course, to live with their families and, in some cases, employers and friends.

The buildings are part of the local people's adaptation to the Maine climate as well as a reflection of the social systems that operated in the area. The structures provide a tangible link to the lives of people who have lived in the Harraseeket district. The majority of the buildings are located in four distinct geographic areas—along the peninsula of Wolf Neck and in the three villages of Mast Landing, Porters Landing, and South Freeport.

The Communities

For about 1,000 years before people attempted to settle year-round along the shores of the Harraseeket

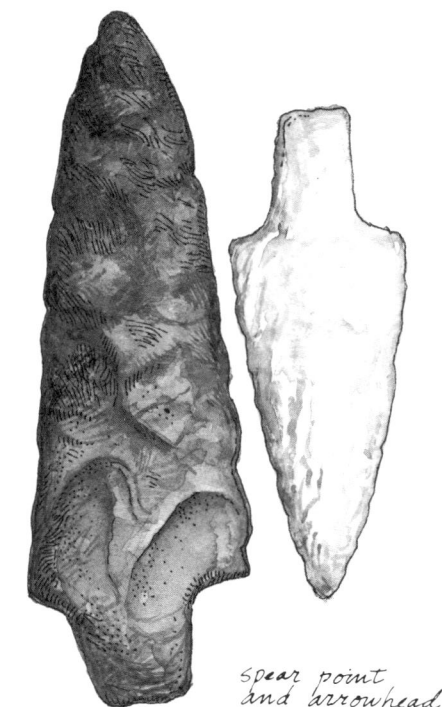

spear point and arrowhead

estuary, the area was frequented by people who stayed only one or two seasons of the year, primarily in search of fish. Little is known about the daily lives of the Indians and early European fishermen who visited the coast of Maine prior to permanent settlement, and there is no specific information about their lives along the Harraseeket. The nature of their social structures, their religious beliefs, their use of natural resources, and much more remain unknown. Hopefully, current archaeological excavations on nearby islands in Casco Bay will produce some clues about past lifestyles.

After the discovery of the New World by the ruling class of Europe, explorers were sent in search of riches, which they found in the wealth of the new land's natural resources. The explorers were followed by settlers who built permanent settlements along the shores of estuaries, first on the islands and then on the mainland. Communities based on the social and economic needs of the permanent settlers began to emerge.

The charter for the town of ancient North Yarmouth, which includes present-day Freeport, Pownal, Yarmouth, North Yarmouth, Cumberland, and Harpswell, was first granted in 1680. A few people settled in what is now Freeport, but the Indian Wars halted any further growth of permanent settlements and almost wiped out both the Indian and European populations of south coastal Maine. At the close of the wars in 1713, settlers returned to ancient North Yarmouth and re-established communities along the shores of the Harraseeket.

After the American Revolution, in 1789, Freeport broke away from ancient North Yarmouth and was established as a town in the Commonwealth of Massachusetts, of which Maine was then a part. During the next one hundred years, Freeport was in the period of its most rapid growth. The population doubled by 1860, growing from 1,330 in 1790 to 2,791. It then leveled off at about 3,000 until the end of the century (doubling again in 1980 to approximately 6,000). It was also during the 1800s that the

shoe workers

settlements of Wolf Neck, Mast Landing, Porters Landing, and South Freeport took shape in a flurry of new construction. Villages formed around the commercial buildings where skilled laborers and their families lived and worked. In rural communities like Wolf Neck, the placement of buildings reflected the needs of farmers and their families.

Several types of communities are found in the Harraseeket district. A community is any interacting group of individuals living in a common location. The Harraseeket district communities discussed so far were centered around the social and economic needs of groups of people. This is the concept of "socio-economic" communities. Ecologists also recognize "biotic" communities, which include *all* life in the area around the Harraseeket. While the socio-economic communities include just people, the biotic communities include people, fish, clams, marsh grass, white pines, and all other coastal life that thrives in the waters and along the shores of the Harraseeket estuary.

Biotic communities can be named for a prominent species in the community, such as the oak-hickory community, or they can be named after the place where the community lives, for example, the mudflat community. Four biotic communities have been identified in the Harraseeket district and named after the places where groups of plants and animals live, interact with each other, and function as a unit. They are the water, mudflat, salt marsh, and upland communities.

None of the communities can stand alone. Each one, with all of its members, is part of a complex system in which all plants and animals interact with each other and their environment.

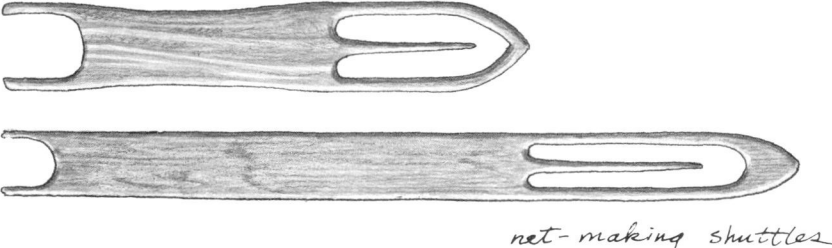

net-making shuttles

Key Words

Harraseeket District - the land, water, and buildings associated with the Harraseeket estuary

Harraseeket Watershed - all of the land that slopes down towards the Harraseeket estuary

Harraseeket Estuary - a semi-enclosed arm of Casco Bay where fresh water mixes with and dilutes the seawater that flows in freely with each high tide

Biotic Community - all plants and animals, including people, that interact as a group in a common location. Examples are upland, salt marsh, mudflat, and water communities.

Socio-economic Community -a group of people interacting to fill social and economic needs in a common location. Examples are Wolf Neck, Mast Landing, Porters Landing, and South Freeport.

Taxonomic Groups - classification of plants and animals by biologist. Examples are phylum, genus, and species.

sugaring

Part II - Guide to the Harraseeket District

1 Wolf Neck

Hussey's Cast Iron Plow
Maine manufacture – 1860

Wolf Neck is a long finger of land, almost surrounded by water, that is covered by a patchwork of field and forest. While traveling along the main road on the Neck, the frequent large fields lead the eye beyond wooden farmhouses toward the water of the Harraseeket estuary to the west, and Casco Bay to the east.

Contrary to what is often thought, Wolf Neck was not named after the wild member of the canine family—the wolf. Instead, the name Wolf refers to Henry Wolfe who lived there with his family in the 1600s. The term "neck" refers to the fact that it is a peninsula.

It can be difficult to imagine Wolf Neck, and other upland areas of the coast, as they were three hundred years ago when people like Henry Wolfe first built year-round homes on land that had previously been used only seasonally by Indians and European fishermen. Prior to year-round settlement, the ancient forests of coastal Maine were a mix of hemlock, white pine, spruce, and balsam fir, along with hardwood species such as oak, hickory, ash, chestnut, birch, maple, beech, and walnut. There may have been some small clearings in the forest. In 1815 Reverend Reuben Nason reported in his "Sketch of Freeport" that many of the tree species that made up the ancient forests were present in Freeport, *"But a small quantity of this wood remains."* Large quantities of hemlock and spruce had been exported from Freeport for spars and for masts of small vessels, according to Reverend Nason. By 1815 there was *"no valuable pine timber in the town... The other kinds of wood (hardwood) have been exported in large quantities to Portland, Boston, and other places for fuel...."* In some cases, the trees were not utilized, but were cut and left to rot or burned in place to clear land for agriculture.

Although the Neck was not named after wolves, the eastern timber wolf was common along the coast during early settlement, and Henry Wolfe and his fellow settlers may have found them on Wolf Neck. They undoubtedly hunted and trapped black bear, fox, raccoon, snowshoe hare, weasel, moose, white-tailed deer, grouse, and numerous other animals that lived in the uplands of the Harraseeket watershed. There are reports of American elk all along the coast from Canada to the Gulf of Mexico as late as 1871. Woodland caribou were also reported in coastal Maine, although, like the elk, they no longer exist here. In 1886, the Commissioners of Fisheries and Game of the State of Maine reported that: *"Of all our game animals the caribou is the most capable of taking care of itself."* In 1906 they reported: *"There are no indications of any caribou in the state."*

A look at the list of the members of the upland communities in the Freeport area, on page 14, indicates the diversity of plants and animals that inhabit the land surrounding the Harraseeket estuary. The list only includes the obvious organisms, however, so it gives an inaccurate picture of the complexity of life in the fields and forests of Wolf Neck. For instance, hunters and others interested in wildlife have taken note of white-tailed deer populations on the Neck for hundreds of years and many residents are aware that deer exist on Wolf Neck. In contrast, few people have an interest in the organisms that live in the dead leaves of the forest floor. Yet these organisms play a vital role in maintaining the productivity of the forest by grinding, chewing, dissolving, and eating more than 2,000 pounds of leaves, twigs, seeds, tree trunks, branches and animal remains that may rain down each year upon an acre of forest floor. The number of organisms in each square foot of the forest floor may be four times as great as the human population of the earth!

Most of the human residents of Wolf Neck in the 1800s were farmers, and the generally flat land and the milder temperatures caused by the nearby seawater still make the Neck attractive for agriculture. In the 1800s, the ocean offered other advantages to coastal farmers, advantages that were not available inland, and people who actively utilized the ocean resources became known as "saltwater" farmers.

The advantages of saltwater farming played a major role in the productivity of Freeport soils, C. Peal points out in his letter to the *Maine Farmer* of June 11, 1863. *"It is so easy to enrich the farms from the ocean, that hay is largely sold. Some 15,000 tons per year go from these wharves, besides large quantities of potatoes."* The saltwater farmer "enriched the farm from the ocean" by spreading large quantities of seaweed, eelgrass, rockweed, and marsh "muck" or mud on their fields. These materials, and other organic material, were either collected on the shore and hauled by the cartful directly to the fields, or stacked in compost piles to be spread after the material had decomposed. Some farmers claimed to have seen beneficial results from spreading marsh muck on their fields for up to twenty years after it was applied.

In addition to a ready-made source of fertilizer, the ocean provided other advantages as well. The salt marsh was a valuable resource that yielded salt hay, an acceptable cattle feed and a good material for animal bedding. The saltwater farmer could fish in the estuary to supplement his income and his family's diet. Long before good roads were built, the nearby ocean was the transportation route to local markets for excess farm and forest products. Life on the saltwater farm was a unique adaptation to the zone where land meets sea.

In the late 1800s, farming on Wolf Neck and in other parts of Freeport evolved into a large scale operation. Local businessman Edmund B. Mallet harvested 300 tons of hay from his 500 acres in

Salt Marsh Hay

1891. It is not known if he used marine fertilizers, but the sea was important in his farming operation, nonetheless. Mr. Mallet built a large pier of granite at his farm on Wolf Neck in order to load hay on vessels headed for distant markets. Today an organic beef farm continues large scale farming on Wolf Neck and still sends products to distant markets, although no longer by sea.

Farming has had a lasting effect on the Wolf Neck landscape. All of the land has been cut-over in the past, either as farmstead woodlots or cleared pasture or cropland. During the 1840s, 1850s, and 1860s, farms were abandoned as residents left for the more fertile fields of the Midwest, the battlefields of the Civil War, and the goldfields of California. Later in the century, many farmers went to work in factories and still more farm fields were abandoned. The present forests on Wolf Neck took seed in the abandoned farm fields and indicate the patterns of past land use.

upland hay

Members of the Wolf Neck Community - 1860 Freeport, Maine

Heads of Households (Number of Occupants)

Ship Joiners
 John D. Mann (9)
Brickmakers
 Anderson Brewer, Jr. (3)
Caulkers
 Lewis Litchfield (10)
Carpenters
 Anderson Brewer (5)
Mariners
 Elias Day (4)
 Elias H. Day (7)
Farmers
 George Aldridge (6)
 Samuel Banks (5)
 Benson Boutelle (3)
 Hezek Brewer (6)
 Joseph Brewer (4)
 William Collins (8)
 Isaac Mann (5)
 James Mann (5)
 John Mann (6)
 Robert Mann (2)
 William Mann (3)
 Josiah Merrill (7)
 Samuel Prithens (8)
 William R. Rogers (8)
 Albion S. Tracy (5)
 N. G. True (8)
 Eben Wilbur (6)
 Samuel Wilbur (4)
No Listed Occupation
 Jane Mann (3)

Abundance of Community Members

Low — High

Category	Count
Schoolchildren (male/female)	38
Farmers (male)	20
Wives (female)	20
Farm Laborers (male)	8
Mariners (male)	4
Ship Joiners (male)	2
Joiners (male)	2
Teachers (male/female)	2
Factory Operators (female)	2
Fishermen (male)	1
Milliners (female)	1
Ship Carpenters (male)	1
Carpenters (male)	1
Brickmakers (male)	1
Caulkers (male)	1
Tailoresses (female)	1

NOTE: *Includes people believed to have lived at Wolf Neck in 1860 based on contemporary maps and deeds and the United States Census. The 1860 Census does not differentiate between the socio-economic communities of the Harraseeket District nor include "wife" as a category reported. "Schoolchildren" indicates people who have attended school within the year.*

spring sowing

Members of the Coastal Uplands Community — 1980s Southern Maine

Taxonomic Group (Number of Species)*

Animal Kingdom

Chordates:

Mammals
humans (1)
deer & moose (2)
hares & rabbits (2)
porcupines (1)
mice, voles & rats (8)
squirrels (5)
woodchucks (1)
bobcats (1)
foxes (2)
coyotes (1)
skunks (1)
weasels (4)
raccoons (1)
bats (8)
moles (2)
shrews (5)

Birds
finches, sparrows, grosbeaks, & buntings (25)
tanagers (1)
blackbirds (6)
weaver finches (1)
warblers (23)
vireos (5)
starlings (1)
shrikes (1)
waxwings (1)
kinglets (1)
thrushes (10)
wrens (4)
creepers (1)
nuthatches (2)
chickadees (2)
jays & crows (3)
swallows (3)
flycatchers (8)
woodpeckers (6)
hummingbirds (1)
goatsuckers (2)
owls (6)
cuckoos (2)
doves (2)
sandpipers (1)
grouse (2)
hawks & falcons (11)

Reptiles
snakes (7)
turtles (1)

Amphibians
frogs (1)
toads (1)
newts (1)
salamanders (6)

Arthropods:

Centipedes (+)

Millipedes (+)

Insects
bees, ants & wasps (+)
fleas (+)
flies (+)
butterflies & moths (+)
caddisflies (+)
scorpionflies (+)
beetles (+)
fishflies, lacewings & antlions (+)
cicadas, leafhoppers & aphids (+)
bugs (+)
thrips (+)
lice (+)
stoneflies (+)
grasshoppers & crickets (+)
dragonflies & damselflies (+)
mayflies (+)
bristletails (+)
springtails (+)

Spiders, Mites & Ticks
garden spiders (+)
daddy longlegs (+)
wolf spiders (+)
ticks (+)
mites (+)

Segmented Worms (+)

Molluscs:
Snails & Slugs (+)

Nematodes (+)

Flatworms (+)

Plant Kingdom

Vascular Plants:

    Flowering plants
        composites (28)
        lobelias (1)
        honeysuckles & viburnums (9)
        bedstraws (12)
        plantains (1)
        broomrapes (2)
        snapdragons (3)
        nightshades (1)
        mints (6)
        milkweeds (1)
        ashes (3)
        primroses (3+)
        heaths (4+)
        dogwoods (2)
        parsleys (3)
        ginsengs (4)
        evening primroses (2)
        loosestrifes (2+)
        violets (2)
        saint john's worts (1)
        grapes (1)
        touch-me-nots (1)
        maples (3)
        bittersweets (1)
        sumacs (2)
        geraniums (1)
        legumes (12)
        roses (15)
        saxifrages (2)
        sundews (2)
        mustards (8)
        barberries (1)
        buttercups (12)
        pinks (4)
        purslanes (3)
        goosefeet (5)
        buckwheats (4)
        birthworts (1)
        nettles (3)
        elms (1)
        oaks (2)
        beeches (1)
        birches (4)
        willows (5)
        orchids (10)
        irises (1)
        lilies (11)
        arums (2)
        sedges (2+)
        grasses (10+)

    Conifers
        junipers (1)
        cedars (1)
        pines (7)
        hemlocks (1)
        spruces (2)
        firs (1)
        yews (1)

    Ferns (23)

    Horsetails (2)

    Club-mosses (4)

    Bryophytes:

        Mosses (60+)

        Liverworts (10+)

    Lichens (20+)

    Algae (+)

Fungus Kingdom

    Lichens (+)

    Fungi:

        Puffballs (+)

        Shelf fungi (+)

        Mushrooms (100+)

    Mildews (+)

    Molds (+)

Protista Kingdom

    Slime-molds (+)

    Amoebas (+)

    Ciliates (+)

Radiolarians (+)

Flagellates (+)

Monera Kingdom

Blue-green Algae (+)

Bacteria (+)

* "(+)" indicates number of species unknown/numerous.

NOTE: Includes terrestrial species selected through personal observations; use of field guides to flora and fauna, and Ecological Characterization of Coastal Maine *(Newton Corner, MA: U.S. Fish and Wildlife Service, October, 1980); and consultations with naturalists. Many coastal Maine species are not represented in the four biotic communities chosen for the text.*

Abundance of Community Members

	Low	High
Bacteria		*
Fungi		*
Slime-molds		*
Molds		*
Nematodes		*
Segmented Worms	*	
Arthropods	*	
Blue-green Algae	*	
Flagellates	*	
Radiolarians	*	
Ciliates	*	
Amoebas	*	
Mildews	*	
Lichens	*	
Algae	*	
Flatworms	*	
Molluscs	*	
Bryophytes	*	
Vascular Plants	*	
Chordates	*	

common garter snake

Profile: Samuel Banks

Samuel Banks

Samuel Banks, who lived in the Pote House in the mid-1800s, was a saltwater farmer. In 1860, Banks was operating the 75 acre farm with his two sons, James and Evan. Forty-five acres of farmland had been cleared for fields, while 30 acres were uncleared and used in part as a wood lot. The Bankses owned cows, oxen, sheep, and pigs, but, like most farmers of their time, did not own horses. Oxen provided farm power, and people traveled on foot or by boat. The farm produced wheat, corn, peas, beans, potatoes, hay, butter, and wool. Banks was one of the few Freeport farmers at that time who still grew his own wheat, a crop ill-suited to the wet, clay soils of southern coastal Maine. Most families preferred to buy flour which was imported by railroad from upstate New York and the Midwest.

By 1870, James and Evan had married and moved to homes of their own in Freeport. James is listed in the census as a *"one-armed soldier,"* a reminder of the conflict over slavery. Banks had retained 44 acres of fields, but the woodland acreage of the farm was reduced to 16 acres. He had cows, oxen, sheep, pigs, and still no horse. Wheat had been replaced by oats and barley. Crops of corn, peas, beans, potatoes, butter, hay, and wool continued to be grown. Banks now had to hire laborers to replace his two sons as he continued to use the resources of both land and sea for his livelihood.

Profile: White Pine

White Pine cone and needles

White pine is a "pioneer species," one of the first trees to invade abandoned farm fields in Southern Maine. It is a sun-loving tree, and old fields act as a natural nursery for its lightweight seeds which drift on the wind. The abundance of white pine on Wolf Neck today comes from pines springing up in abandoned farm fields. In many areas of Freeport, fields that have not been mowed recently are dotted with small pines—the process is still going on today. If they grow in the open, pines are symmetrical. In older forests like Wolf Neck Woods State Park, pines grow to be very tall, up to 100 feet, with branches occurring only at the top where sunlight is available.

The bark of old trees is dark, with broad ridges, and is about 1 to 2 inches thick. When the tree is young, the bark is smooth, thin, and green, tinted with reddish brown. Pine needles grow 3 to 5 inches long and are arranged in clusters of five. They are bluish-green in color and have a strip of white on one side. The brown cones grow from 4 to 8 inches long and take two years to mature.

The eastern white pine was growing in the ancient forests when Europeans first arrived in the Harraseeket watershed, although it was not as common as it is today. Early explorers recognizing the value of New World forests returned home with fantastic tales about the abundant natural resources, including the white pine. The British Admiralty was particularly interested in the pines as a source of masts and spars for the extensive fleet of the Royal Navy. As early as 1685 all great pines suitable for the Admiralty's use were reserved by the crown as masts. Colonists were forbidden to cut these trees. Before long all of the large pines in places like Freeport were cut by the King's agents—or by poachers.

    Throughout the 1700s and 1800s, pines were important to the commercial growth of the area. Pine wood is light in weight and color, very durable, straight-grained, and easily worked. It was ideal for the building of floors and household interiors as well as furniture. The wide boards cut from old growth trees made big jobs go quickly. Pine was also important in building ships and small craft. The characteristic shape of the banks dories that were used so extensively in the fishing fleets on the Grand Banks evolved as a result of the wide pine boards that formed their planking.

White Pine

On Your Own on Wolf Neck

Saltwater Farm: To reach Wolf Neck by land take Bow Street, opposite L.L. Bean's retail salesroom, and follow the signs toward Wolf Neck Woods State Park. Just before arriving at the Park on Wolf Neck Road, you will see the Pote House on the left. It is the first house after the intersection with the Burnett Road. The Pote House was a saltwater farmhouse throughout the 1800s. Samuel Banks lived in this house in the 1860s and 1870s. It is currently a private residence, so please respect the owner's privacy. The connection between the farm and the ocean is obvious; its fields slope down to Casco Bay. A panel by the roadside explains some of the history of the house and mentions Captain Greenfield Pote after whom it was named.

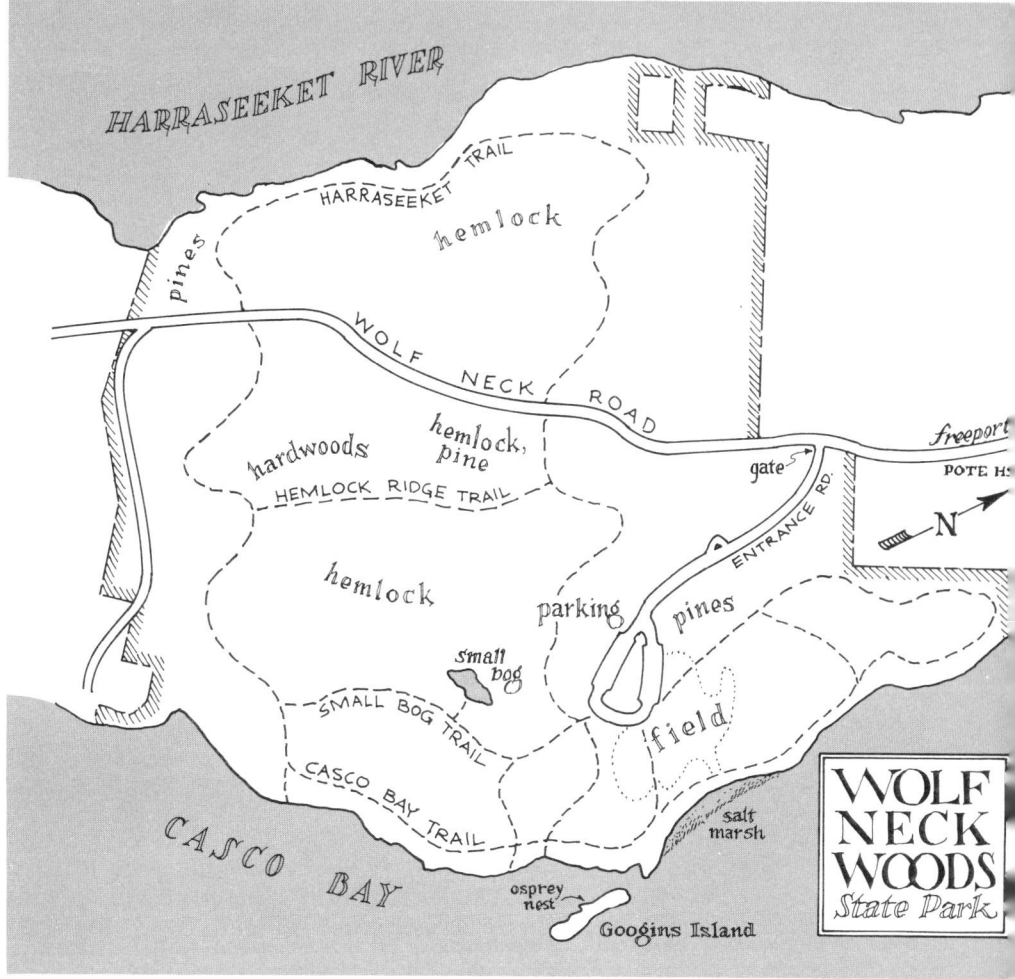

Wolf Neck Woods State Park:
Just beyond the Pote House is the entrance to Wolf Neck Woods State Park, open daily from dawn to dusk. A fee is charged to visit the park from Memorial Day through Labor Day. During the winter the gate will be closed, but you can park your car on the east side of Wolf Neck Road and walk or ski into the Park.

Harraseeket Trail: Start at the map signboard (not mounted during the winter) in the parking area and follow the trail to the Harraseeket estuary, about an hour for the full loop. Notice that the kinds of plants change as you travel along the trail. Factors such as soil, competition from other plants, and the distance from the shore determine where plants will grow. The time that has passed since cleared fields were mowed or burned also helps determine changing patterns of growth. An area along the trail that was field until 40 years ago is now a forest of mixed hardwoods and conifers. Further along the trail you will enter a forest of tall pines which was a cleared area at one time. It has been forest for about 100 years. Do you see any trees that would make a straight, tall mast for a ship? Notice that you cross a ridge as you enter the pine forest. This is the eastern boundary of the Harraseeket watershed. The land between the parking area and the ridge drains directly into Casco Bay. The land along the trail from the ridge to the shore of the Harraseeket drains into the estuary. South Freeport is visible from the trail as it follows the shore of the Harraseeket. Some old stone fences and young pine stands indicate the former sites of other old fields along the trail.

Century Pine Bark Rubbings:
After walking five to ten minutes from the parking area along the Harraseeket Trail, look for a stand of old-growth pine. Both white pine and red pine grow along the stretch of trail where it crosses the Wolf Neck Road. The trees directly across the road, to the west, are red pines, easily identified by their reddish bark. Several large white pines, with greyish bark, are 25-30 feet to the right, or north, of where the trail crosses the road. Several of these majestic trees are over 100 years old. How many arms around is a "century pine?"

In order to make a bark rubbing of a pine you will need several large pieces of strong paper, two or three crayons without their paper wrappers, and several thumbtacks. Tack the paper securely to the tree, rub a crayon on its side across the paper and the pattern of the bark will appear. The bark of younger pines may be easier to record. Try a red pine and a white pine. Put several designs on a single piece of paper. You can also do a rubbing of the needles to complete your record of a pine by spreading the needles on a rock or other hard surface and rubbing the crayon over them.

Programs: The park offers year-round programs and guided walks for the public. Announcements in local papers and signs posted in the park list the time and topic of these programs. Self-guiding brochures are available at the park entrance. The Casco Bay Trail is one of the most popular in the park; following the shore of the Bay, it takes visitors past the resident osprey nest on Googins Island.

Osprey

2 Mast Landing

two-man crosscut saw

Many Freeport residents pass through Mast Landing regularly without realizing that it was one of the most important settlements in Freeport in the early 1800s. Then known as Harraseeket Landing, it included a school, general store, shoe shop, brickyard, woodworking shop, and other buildings used for housing and commerce. It is located at the inland end of the Harraseeket estuary.

The current name, Mast Landing, is used because, according to legend, large white pines were cut nearby, rafted down the Harraseeket, and loaded onto ships bound for England during the masting trade of the 1700s. To date there is no evidence to document this belief in pre-revolutionary trade. Possibly the name originated during the shipbuilding boom of the 1850s and 1860s when masts and other spars were needed at the downstream settlements of Porters Landing and South Freeport. A few vessels were built at the landing.

Throughout the 1800s, the Harraseeket was the major transportation link with the rest of the world for residents of Mast Landing. Boats came and went with the tide, carrying away items produced in the local brickyard, mills, and workshops, and bringing in a variety of goods wanted by the families of the craftsmen, farmers, laborers, and seafarers who lived in the area. The 1854 day book for the Curtis store, located at Mast Landing, lists transactions for the following items: shoes, eggs, potatoes, coats, gingham, screws, crackers, tea, hats, vests, tobacco, brooms, and various other dry goods.

Above the landing, at what is presently Mast Landing Sanctuary, a stream falls 17 feet to the salt marsh below. The stream and the salt marsh were both important to the development of Mast Landing. The stream was the site of several mills where raw materials were processed with the help of water-driven machinery—an advantage not available on the farm. A sluiceway channeled water from behind a dam directly to the four mills that operated on the stream: two gristmills, a sawmill, and a fulling mill.

It is not known when mills were first built on the stream, but in 1795, interest in property *"commonly known as Dennison's Mills"* was transferred from Stephen Knights and Elijah Haskell to Timothy Dennison. Seven years later, a deed from Dennison records a *"lower gristmill"* and an *"upper gristmill"* at the site. Typically, the gristmills would have ground cornmeal, plaster, animal feed, and perhaps, gunpowder. Flour may have been ground, but poor grain crops, the availability of flour grown and processed in the American Midwest, and the term *"gristmill"* rather than *"flouring mill"* in Mast Landing deeds, suggest that it was not a major activity. The Hadley Falls Company of Holyoke, Massachusetts purchased a *"Grist Mill and Plaster Mill"* at Mast Landing in 1856 along with another mill, *"being used for sawing, planing and turning wood and timber."* The sawmill was invaluable for the Mast Landing Community since it provided a local source of boards and timbers for building houses and boats. Nearby was the fulling mill where cloth

millstone

woven from local wool would have been processed. The material resulting from the hammering and shrinking process was tighter than could be produced on home looms. A dye house operated in conjunction with the mill. There is also mention of a tide mill operating here in the 1800s, but it too is gone. As was often the case, the mills at Mast Landing were owned by several people in shares of 1/8's or 1/16's, thereby sharing the expenses and the profits of the mills.

The Mill Stream is important in the story of Mast Landing for additional reasons. For centuries it has been the home for fur-bearing mammals, including muskrats and beaver, and for freshwater fish—both of which were harvested for human use. Finally, it has also been a major source of the freshwater that mixes with the seawater of Casco Bay to create the Harraseeket estuary. This steady source of freshwater has attracted fish such as alewives, smelt, tommycod, and eels that move between fresh and salt water to spawn.

Gradually, during the 1800s, the need for local mills on the Mill Stream passed. Local goods were replaced by imported items such as the inexpensive wool and cotton cloth woven by the factory textile industry. When the mills burned in the early 1860s, they were not rebuilt. Today, fossil fuels have to a large extent replaced water power, although there is a renewed interest in using hydro power to produce electricity. Along the Maine coast many falls like those at Mast Landing Sanctuary remain abandoned. As technology changes, human use of natural resources changes as well.

Like all of the settlements of the Harraseeket watershed, Mast Landing had its own cemetery in the 1800s. In the past, death was a more acknowledged part of life. The local cemetery provided a constant reminder to all who passed by that their time in this world was short. The oldest marked grave in the Mast Landing Cemetery is that of Mary Dennison who died in 1784. We know little of Mary's life except that she was married to Captain Abner Dennison who probably built the mills at Mast Landing. Joel Kelsey and his wife Susan are also buried there, along with her parents.

Several of the headstones in the cemetery were carved about 1790 by Noah Pratt who lived on the Pleasant Hill Road. Pratt came from a family of stonecutters in Massachusetts and spent a few years in Freeport after the Revolution. It is believed that Noah Pratt carved the Dennison stones. Captain Dennison's epitaph is barely visible today on a weathered headstone, one of the few in the cemetery that appears to be of local material. The

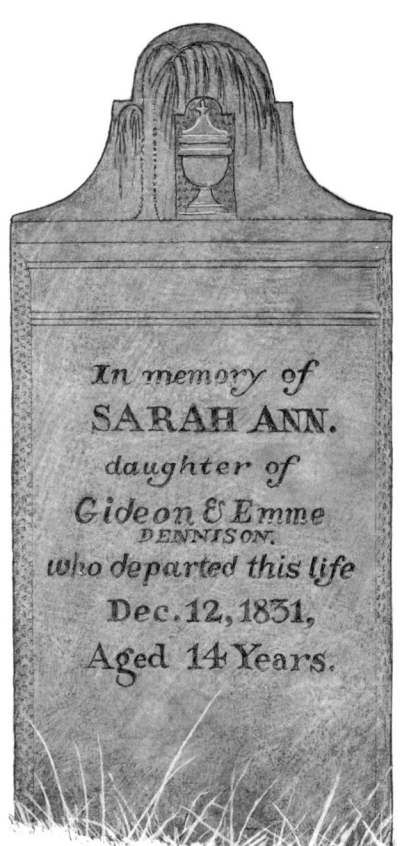

marble and slate imported to the area after his burial retain their carved messages much more clearly. However, the persistent observer can make out the following on Captain Dennison's weathered stone:

Remember this you passerby
As you are now so wonce was I
As I am so Must you be
Prepare for death, [O] follow me

An important feature of Mast Landing is the salt marsh community. The tides regularly flood the marsh producing an environment rich with life. Although only a few plant species can tolerate the salt water of the marsh, spartina grasses have developed the ability to thrive in this environment. These grasses provide a sheltered home for other marsh life. Insects and small fish can often be found in the marsh's tidal pools, and certain varieties of wrens and sparrows build their nests hidden in the spartina grasses. The grasses also offer protection to rodents that in turn attract owls, hawks, and foxes. Raccoons and mink visit the marsh to dig for clams and crabs. The mink might even build nests on the high marsh and become semi-permanent residents.

Until the present century, the salt marsh was considered a valuable resource. No doubt Indians hunted the muskrat, fox, and other small mammals that frequented the marsh. European settlers often chose sites for their villages because of a nearby salt marsh. Marshland was considered so desirable to own that many towns divided it among the original settlers. Often the salt marsh was the only unforested land in a new township. Its grass could be used to thatch the roofs of small buildings, to bed animals, and to feed cattle, both as hay in winter and pasturage in summer.

Once again, changing technology altered human use of the environment. In an industrial society people viewed salt marshes as nothing more than dumping grounds. Road building, filling, pollution, and coastal development permanently changed, and in some cases eliminated, salt marsh communities along the coast. Only recently have people come to realize the value of salt marshes as complex and unique systems and taken steps to preserve them through legislation and education.

red fox

Members of the Mast Landing Community - 1860 Freeport, Maine

Heads of Households (Number of Occupants)

Shipmasters
  J. W. Richardson (6)
Merchants
  Joel Kelsey (4)
Ship Carpenters
  Simeon Curtis (2)
  John D. Ring (8)
Carpenters
  Graham Randall (5)
Brickmakers
  James E. Frank (2)
Caulkers
  Edwin Townsend (2)
  William W. Wilson (4)
Stevedores
  Ruben Curtis (5)
Mariners
  John Dennison (4)
  Tristram Griffing (7)
  John Pierce (3)
Farmers
  Daniel Bartol (3)
  Daniel Curtis (8)
  David Cushing (5)
  Benjamin Dennison (9)
  Freeman Lapham (5)
  Daniel Randall (9)
  B.F.B. Stevens (6)
Farm Laborers
  Hiram Allen (2)
No Listed Occupation
  Emma Dennison (6)

Abundance of Community Members

Category	Low — High
Schoolchildren *(male/female)*	23
Farmers *(male)*	8
Wives *(female)*	7
Mariners *(male)*	5
Joiners *(male)*	3
Ship Carpenters *(male)*	2
Caulkers *(male)*	2
Stevedores *(male)*	2
Brickmakers *(male)*	2
Farm Laborers *(male)*	2
Coopers *(male)*	1
Shoemakers *(male)*	1
Carpenters *(male)*	1
Shipmasters *(male)*	1
Merchants *(male)*	1
Dressmakers *(female)*	1

NOTE: Includes people believed to have lived at Mast Landing in 1860 based on contemporary maps and deeds and the United States Census. The 1860 Census does not differentiate between the socio-economic communities of the Harraseeket District nor include "wife" as a category reported. "Schoolchildren" indicates people who have attended school within the year.

hay fork

Members of the Salt Marsh Grass Community — 1980s Maine

Taxonomic Group (Number of Species)*

Animal Kingdom
Chordates:
- **Mammals**
  - humans (1)
  - deer (1)
  - small rodents (4)
  - foxes (2)
  - skunks (1)
  - weasels (2)
  - raccoons (1)

- **Birds**
  - sparrows (4)
  - blackbirds (2)
  - swallows (3)
  - doves (2)
  - gulls & terns (10)
  - sandpipers (15)
  - plovers (5)
  - rails (2)
  - falcons & hawks (7)
  - geese & ducks (8)
  - ibises (1)
  - herons, egrets, & bitterns (6)

- **Fishes**
  - sticklebacks (4)
  - killifishes (1)
  - eels (1)

Arthropods:
- **Insects**
  - horseflies & deerflies (2+)
  - midges (1)
  - mosquitos (1)
  - craneflies (2)
  - beetles (2)
  - bugs (12+)
  - crickets (1)
  - dragonflies (1)

- **Spiders & Mites** (15+)

- **Crustaceans**
  - crabs (2+)
  - hermit crabs (2)
  - amphipods (+)
  - isopods (+)

Segmented Worms (5)

Molluscs:
- **Snails** (2)
- **Clams** (2)

Ribbonworms (+)

Flatworms (+)

Plant Kingdom
Flowering Plants:
- **Composites** (3)
- **Figworts** (1)
- **Cinquefoils** (1)
- **Sea Lavenders** (1)
- **Pinks** (1)
- **Goosefeet** (2)
- **Rushes** (1)
- **Sedges** (5)
- **Grasses** (6)
- **Plantains** (1)
- **Cattails** (1)

Algae: (10+)

Protista Kingdom
Ciliates: (+)

Radiolarians: (+)

Flagellates: (+)

Monera Kingdom
  Blue-green Algae (+)

  Bacteria (+)

Abundance of Community Members

```
                        Low                           High
Ciliates                _____*
Bacteria                _____*
Blue-green Algae        _____*
Flagellates             _____*
Algae                   _____*
Molluscs                _____*
Radiolarians            _____*
Segmented Worms         _____*
Arthropods              _____*
Flowering Plants        *
Flatworms               *
Ribbonworms             *
Chordates               *
```

* "(+)" indicates number of species unknown/numerous.

NOTE: Includes organisms commonly inhabitating marine peat and shallow salt marsh pools, and the animals that fed on them there. Species selection based on personal observation; Ecological Characterization of Coastal Maine (Newton Corner, MA: U.S. Fish and Wildlife Service, October, 1980); and consultation with biologists. Many coastal Maine species are not represented in the four biotic communities chosen for the text.

Dragonfly

Profile: Joel Kelsey

Joel Kelsey of Mast Landing, farmer, merchant and brickmaker, epitomized the nineteenth-century businessman who depended upon natural resources. He was involved in several businesses that extensively used the resources of the Harraseeket estuary. Most men in the nineteenth century were farmers at least part of the time, and Kelsey was no exception. In the 1850s and 1860s, he had a 70- to 80-acre farm that produced potatoes, peas, beans, corn, oats, barley, butter, and hay. In addition, he had a horse, oxen, and cows.

Kelsey also used other Harraseeket resources. He and his son, John, owned a brickyard at Mast Landing which employed four men in 1850. The clay for the brick was dug from the marine clay deposits along the estuary. In this one year, the brickyard used 140 cords of wood taken from local forests for firing 400,000 bricks.

Kelsey owned many acres of salt marsh. The marsh produced valuable patens grass, grown effortlessly because no seeding or land clearing was required. Kelsey could harvest the grass for use on his farm or to send to market. Frequently, harvesting rights to the marshes were rented out to farmers, and the marsh owner would collect rent in cash or in salt hay. Marshes could be diked to control the flooding by the saltwater, thereby regulating the type of grass grown. The remains of old dikes, possibly built by Joel Kelsey, can still be seen on the salt marshes of the Harraseeket.

Joel Kelsey was also part owner of the Mast Landing fulling mill. Cloth woven from locally produced wool was processed here. Whether it was the farmland, marine clay, salt grass or woodland resources, all were utilized by Kelsey to provide himself and his family with the necessities, as well as some luxuries, of life.

Profile: Spartina Grasses

Saltwater cordgrass
Spartina Alterniflora

Salt marsh hay
Spartina Patens

Two types of spartina grass, *Spartina alterniflora* and *Spartina patens*, grow in the salt marsh at Mast Landing. *Alterniflora* is a very coarse grass often called thatch, or cordgrass, by coastal farmers. It was used in the early colonial period to thatch the roofs of small buildings and, until the 1900s, to provide bedding materials for animals. *Patens* is a much finer grass that grows in a swirl pattern on the marsh. From the time of first settlement to the late 1800s, this grass was considered a valuable natural resource. Although not as nutritious as hay grown on uplands, salt marsh hay made from *Spartina patens* was an acceptable winter feed for cattle. In summer, cattle were often pastured on the marsh, and one can still see the remains of abandoned fencing on many salt marshes.

The salt marsh is flooded regularly with saltwater, and even at low tide the roots of many marsh grasses are still in contact with saltwater. Most plants could not live in this environment, but the spartina grasses have developed unique adaptive mechanisms. Unlike most other plants, the water inside the spartina grasses has a higher salt concentration than the water of the estuary. Therefore, the plant is able to absorb more water and nutrients as needed. If the concentrations of salt were greater in the seawater, water would be drawn out of the spartina grasses and they would die, as do most other plants when exposed to saltwater. Although there are other plant species that do grow in the salt marsh, the spartina grasses dominate this environment.

On Your Own at Mast Landing

Mast Landing Village: Mast Landing is located on Bow Street about 1 mile from the L.L. Bean retail salesroom. The buildings that made up the active commercial village of the 1800s no longer mark the site, but there is still much to see here.

Pull off Bow Street at the public boat landing, marked by a small information panel opposite Upper Mast Landing Road. The first thing you will notice is the marsh itself. It is an ideal habitat for many animals, and it was an oasis in a forested wilderness to the first settlers who used the marsh for pastures and hayfields. Walk around the marsh, watching for wet spots, noting the characteristic "cowlick" swirls of the salt hay *Spartina patens*. Along the banks of the estuary, only the tough, taller cordgrass or thatch (*Spartina alterniflora*) survives.

Try to imagine small sailing vessels tied up to a wharf, bringing supplies, and being loaded with lumber, firewood, bricks, and flour. The remains of the wharf and discarded bricks can be seen on the opposite bank of the Harraseeket at low tide. Just across the stream next to the road is the large two-and-a-half story house in which Joel Kelsey lived. The main residential area of the community still stands on the hill above the landing: modest Cape Cod homes built when the village was at its peak of prosperity in the early 1800s.

Mast Landing Sanctuary: Drive from the landing one-tenth of a mile up Upper Mast Landing Road to the Mast Landing Sanctuary. The sanctuary is owned and maintained by the Maine Audubon Society and is open to the public from dawn to dusk every day of the year. Although no fee is charged to visit the Sanctuary, a donation is requested from visitors.

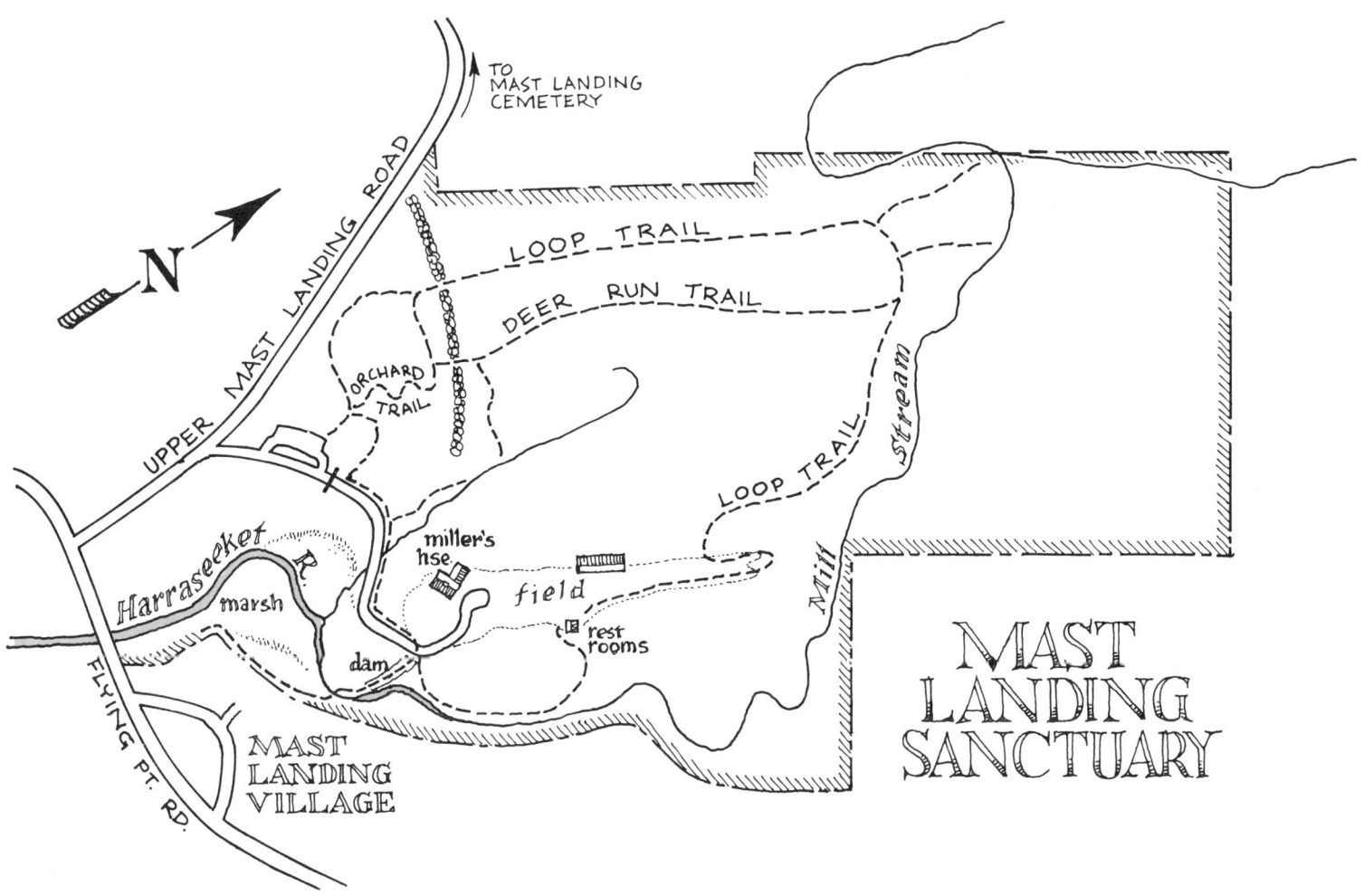

Falls and Millsite: The remains of several mills can still be seen at Mast Landing Sanctuary. The dam, built of field and quarrystone, is mostly intact, but the stream has changed its course and now flows around the end of the dam. Walk down the service road to the salt marsh, which is tide level—the head of the Harraseeket estuary. Look at the falls which tumble some 17 feet from the high ground above. Migrating fish, such as alewives, congregate at these falls during spawning, and the site remains a fishing spot for mammals and birds during the fishes' seasonal migrations. Attracted by the good fishing, a Great Blue Heron can almost always be seen in the vicinity during the warmer months.

As you walk up the hill to the dam, consider the potential energy in the waterfall. The early residents utilized the waterfall because it was one of the few sources of harnessable power in the days before steam engines and electricity. There was a price to be paid for power, however, as there is today. Think of the time and human and animal energy required to quarry the large granite blocks, transport them to the damsite, and move them into position for the dam and building foundations. How many mill foundations can you spot? Can you see the remains of the town road which once passed below the dam to the miller's house on the hill?

Miller's House: In the 1800s skilled workers also grew much of their own food, therefore the miller's house was also a farmhouse. After the last mill burned in 1861, farming became the principal activity on the property. A few signs of agricultural activity remain. Notice the addition, or "ell" on the house, which was used for storage and farm work. A large barn, since destroyed, housed animals and hay nearby.

A few apple trees from the orchard have survived, and some of the fields and pastures which have been mowed regularly have not yet been reclaimed by the forest. Watch for the stone walls which once fenced the fields and pastures as you explore the upland environment of the 100-acre sanctuary. Yellow and blue markers lead you on the Sanctuary Loop Trail. Blue markers indicate the shortest route to the parking area.

Cellar Hole: Follow the Loop Trail from the parking area. You will pass through an abandoned orchard being taken over by sun-loving pines. Shortly you will come to an old stone wall and a small clearing. Look for a pair of cedars, conical evergreen trees, and for raspberry bushes that mark an old house foundation. Stop by the cellar hole and sit quietly by yourself. Records of who built the house that stood on this site, or of when it was built, are not available. As you sit on the edge of the cellar hole, imagine how this small field has changed since people lived and worked here 100 or 150 years ago. Imagine the family here. Did any of them go to sea? How was the land used? Was the stone wall important? What did the barn look like that stood nearby? Often cellars were not built under the entire house; how large do you think the house was that stood here? Create a picture of the house and barn in your mind and, if you brought some paper, draw your image of the past. Thinking of the present and who you are, how is your life different from the people you imagined living here? If you like, write down some of your thoughts.

Mill dam at Mast Landing

Mast Landing Cemetery: One-half mile above the Sanctuary on Upper Mast Landing Road is the cemetery where many of the early residents of Mast Landing are buried. Adequate parking is not available at the cemetery, so you may want to leave your car in the Sanctuary parking area and walk. Follow the Loop Trail through the stone wall, and then turn left onto an old dirt road to Upper Mast Landing Road. The cemetery will be within sight as you walk a few steps to the right along the paved road.

The stonecutters of the 1800s created an enduring record of the statistics of life and death at Mast Landing, as well as of the hopes and beliefs of people who lived here. There are epitaphs which record fragments of the deceased's life on earth or their hopes for eternal life. Symbols on the tombstones also tell a story. There are three symbols at Mast Landing Cemetery that appear with regularity in burial grounds throughout New England. The death's head reminds all who pass of the certainty of death. The urn represents the soul arising out of the ashes of death. The willow is a symbol of mourning and renewed life. Look for the symbols and discover the time periods when they were popular at Mast Landing. Examine the names and birth and death dates of the persons in the cemetery. AE is an abbreviation of the Latin *Aetalis*, or years of life. What does it tell you about life in the Mast Landing community for men, women, and children? What was their life expectancy? What is suggested about their religious spirit? Collectively, what do the tombstones indicate about the development of the community of Mast Landing? When was the last person buried here?

Mast Landing cemetery

3 Porters Landing

auger

Porters Landing, located on the northwest arm of the estuary, was an early shipbuilding center and docking facility. Seward Porter and his sons, Seward and Samuel, built vessels at Porters Landing during the early 1800s. The *Dash*, a famous privateer built at the Porter yard, harrassed and outran British ships during the War of 1812. When not pursuing enemy vessels, the *Dash* made trips to Puerto Rico to exchange New England produce, probably lumber, for coffee.

The British were but one of the hazards the ship and crew encountered at sea. Frequent storms and contrary winds could also cause problems. In the *Dash* log book, on February 14, 1814, Master Killeran reported the following storm:

Those 24 hours comences with a hard gale at NW with squalls of snow & verry cold. . . . at 3 a sea struck her on the larboard bow and stove in the bulworks shifted the cargo in at am the gale abates . . . . found she had two streaks list, all hands employed in shifting coffee in the fore hold found considerable of the Cargo & freight damaged the water had blown thro the seiling quite up to the deck—

The next day Killeran was able to report "*arrived safe at Portland all well.*" Not all trips ended so happily. A few years later, the *Dash* was lost at sea, taking several Freeport men down with the vessel.

The daily tides have regulated human activity at Porters Landing, and elsewhere along the Harraseeket, for centuries. The comings and goings of vessels, the gathering of shellfish, or the launching of new ships were dictated by the tides. Surely the tides played an important role on the day in 1859 when the last ship launched from Porters Landing was eased into the shallow waters there. Built by Rufus Soule and his son Rufus C. Soule, who had operated a shipyard at Porters Landing since the 1840s, the 1,150 ton *Daniel L. Choate* marked the end of an era for the Porters Landing community. The exact chain of events which brought about the closing of the Porters Landing shipyards over 125 years ago is not known, but competition from the active South Freeport yards, where there was deeper water, was undoubtedly a factor. The deeper water at South Freeport provided competition for the other major economic activity at Porters Landing as well — shipping.

In 1770, Cumberland County built a road from Porters Landing to Freeport Village (the present South Street) which then continued to the Androscoggin River in Durham. John Cushing moved his family over this road in April of 1790.

"Removed from Durham to Freeport, and a most tremendous time through mud and water; arrived at Mr. Porter's in the evening." The next day they continued by boat to their new farm at Stockbridge Point, according to Cushing's diary.

South Street linked Porters Landing to the inland markets of the Androscoggin River Valley and made it a major trade center in the early 1800s. Then, in 1830, the road was extended to South Freeport, with its access to deeper water. Finally, in 1849, new competition arrived for shipping at Porters Landing — the railroad came to Freeport Village.

A channel was dredged in an attempt to keep Porters Landing competitive as a trade center. E. B. Mallett stated his case in support of the dredging in a letter of January, 1884, printed in the *Report of the Chief of Engineers, U.S. Army:*

> I have over 100,000 paving stone all cut and ready to ship as soon as the season opens. I want to ship these by water, but can not; shall have to ship by rail. Then I have a party who stands ready to establish a coal yard to the head of navigation, and he will do so as soon as loaded vessels can come up [to the landing].

A channel was dredged in 1896 and the results of the dredging are still apparent today. The channel can be seen from the air and two piles of stones south of Bartol Island, "dolphins" or channel markers, are a puzzle to many modern-day boaters.

At first glance, the mud flats at Porters Landing seem lifeless, but this first impression is far from the truth. Microscopic algae grow on the flats attracting animals which feed on them. Snails, clams, mussels, worms, and smaller microscopic animals are permanent residents of the flats. In addition, fish, crabs and birds forage back and forth over the flats with the rising and falling of the tides.

The daily rhythm of the tides has a dramatic impact on all creatures in the mud flats at Porters Landing. Only plants and animals which can cope with being covered by cold, salty seawater twice a day and then being exposed to the hot summer sun or scraped by chunks of ice in the winter, have survived. While there are relatively few species living in the mud flat community compared to the other biotic communities in the Harraseeket watershed, there are many more species of plants and animals than most people are familiar with, as can be seen on page 42. Because there are literally billions of individuals of each species, the mud flats are actually full of life.

39

Members of the Porters Landing Community - 1860 Freeport, Maine

Heads of Households (Number of Occupants)

Merchants
 Charles H. Pettengill (9)
Master Carpenters
 George C. Soule (8)
Blacksmiths
 Stephen Anderson (5)
Ship Carpenters
 John Blithen (5)
 Daniel Brewer (3)
 William G. Brewer (3)
 Thomas Chase (6)
 Edwin B. Grant (3)
Ship Joiners
 Freeman Means (4)
Caulkers
 Charles Litchfield (4)
Joiners
 Charles W. Soule (3)
 Isaac S. Soule (2)
House Joiners
 George Brewer (4)
Shoemakers
 Joshua Soule (4)
Coopers
 Samuel Lunt (4)
House Carpenters
 Edward Melcher (10)
 John A. Osgood (8)
Mariners
 Nehimeah Brewer (4)
 Isaac Lambert (6)
 Joseph Mann (4)

Farmers
 Daniel Grant (6)
 John S. Sherman (3)
 Rufus C. Soule (5)
Painters
 William M. Curtis (8)
Laborers
 Simon Bragden (6)
No Listed Occupation
 Elizabeth Staples (3)

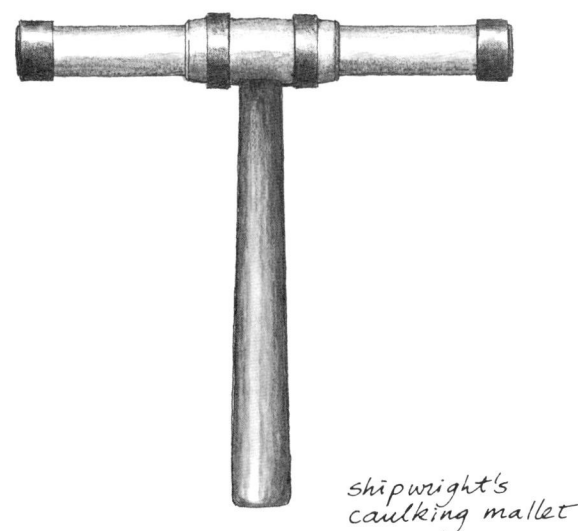

shipwright's caulking mallet

Abundance of Community Members

	Low	High
Schoolchildren *(male/female)*		38
Wives *(female)*		25
Farmers *(male)*	7	
Ship Carpenters *(male)*	6	
Mariners *(male)*	4	
Joiners *(male)*	4	
Shoemakers *(male)*	2	
House Carpenters *(male)*	2	
Shipbuilders *(male)*	2	
Ship Joiners *(male)*	1	
House Joiners *(male)*	1	
Miners *(male)*	1	
Factory Operators *(female)*	1	
Blacksmiths *(male)*	1	
Laborers *(male)*	1	
Painters *(male)*	1	
Caulkers *(male)*	1	
Master Carpenters *(male)*	1	
Merchants *(male)*	1	
Clerks *(male)*	1	
Coopers *(male)*	1	
Carpenters *(male)*	1	
Milliners *(female)*	1	
Tailoresses *(female)*	1	

NOTE: *Includes people believed to have lived at Porters Landing in 1860 based on contemporary maps and deeds and the United States Census. The 1860 Census does not differentiate between the socio-economic communities of the Harraseeket District nor include "wife" as a category reported. "Schoolchildren" indicates people who have attended school within the year.*

grain cradle

Members of the Intertidal Mud flat Community — 1980s Maine

Taxonomic Group (Number of Species)*

Animal Kingdom

Chordates:

Mammals
humans (1)
muskrats (1)
otters (1)
raccoons (1)

Birds
crows (2)
gulls (5)
sandpipers (12)
plovers (5)
rails (2)
ducks (8)
ibises (1)
herons, egrets & bitterns (6)

Fishes (52)
See: "Members of the Estuarine Water Community"

Arthropods:

Horseshoe crabs (1)

Insects
midges (2)
sandflies (2)
beetles (1)
springtails (1)

Crustaceans
green crabs (1)
hermit crabs (2)
amphipods (4+)
isopods (+)

Molluscs:

Snails
periwinkles (2)
hydrobias (+)

Bivalves
clams (2)
mussels (2)

Echiuran Worms (+)

Roundworms (+)

Ribbonworms (+)

Segmented Worms (+)

Flatworms (3)

Plant Kingdom

Seed Plants:

Eel grass (1)

Seaweeds:

Sea lettuce (1)

Diatoms (20+)

Dinoflagellates (+)

Protista Kingdom

Ciliates (+)

Radiolarians (+)

Flagellates (+)

Monera Kingdom

Blue-green Algae (+)

Bacteria (+)

*"(+)" indicates number of species unknown/numerous.

NOTE: Includes resident and transient adult organisms that feed at or below the surface of inter-tidal mud flats in estuaries. Species selection based on personal observations; Ecological Characterization of Coastal Maine *(Newton Corner, MA: U.S. Fish and Wildlife Service, October, 1980)*; and consultation with biologists. Many coastal Maine species are not represented in the four biotic communities chosen for the text.

Abundance of Community Members

```
                        Low                    High
                        |_____|

Bacteria                _____*
Blue-green Algae        _____*
Flagellates             _____*
Ciliates                _____*
Diatoms                 _____*
Dinoflagellates         _____*
Segmented Worms         _____*
Ribbonworms             _____*
Molluscs                _____*
Radiolarians            _____*
Seaweeds                _____*
Flatworms               _____*
Roundworms              _____*
Echiuran Worms          _____*
Arthropods              ____*
Chordates               *
```

Killdeer

43

Profile: Soft-shelled Clam

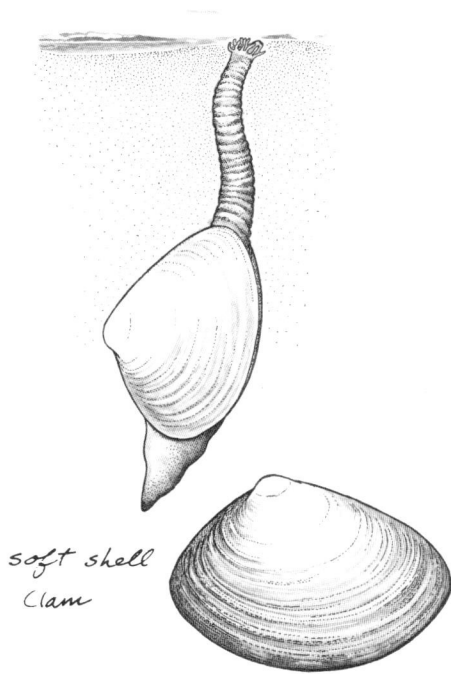

soft shell clam

Soft-shelled clams live year-round in mud flats like those at Porters Landing. These small, but hardy, creatures can survive in temperatures ranging from 30 degrees to 80 degrees Fahrenheit; can withstand a wide range of salt concentrations; and can adjust to alternatively wet or dry conditions caused by the coming and going of the tides.

The clam has a hinged shell which is generally white and smooth in sandy flats with lots of oxygen, and gray and rough in rocky and clay flats where there is less oxygen. The age of a clam can be roughly determined by counting the number of rings on the shell. Each ring marks a slowing in the clam's growth, usually due to severe conditions every winter.

A foot that can be extended from or drawn into the shell enables clams to move. As juveniles, clams may crawl along the surface of the flats and be swept along with water currents. Once they are adults, they generally move up or down in one spot in the mud.

Clams feed on small plants and animals brought to the flats by the tides. Those living closer to the low water mark are covered with saltwater for longer periods each day providing more feeding time than their relatives living near the high tide mark. Subsequently, they grow more quickly.

Clams are threatened by many predators throughout their lives. As juveniles, tiny shrimp-like animals and worms eat them. As they grow larger, mummichogs (a small fish), moonsnails, crabs, and mammals, such as raccoons, devour them. Particularly in southern Maine, green crabs have consumed whole populations of clams. Finally, as 2-4 inch adults, clams burrow deeply enough to evade most predators, except humans, who traditionally have harvested adult clams in Maine. The location of clams is revealed by the small air holes that are visible in the mud.

Profile: John Blethen

John Blethen lived with his wife Lavinia and their large family at Porters Landing where he operated a shipbuilding business in the mid-1800s. In 1850, Blethen employed five men who earned, collectively, an average of $200 per month. To build a wooden sailing vessel, Blethen and his crew had to use many raw materials such as iron, copper, paint, canvas duck for sails, cordage for rigging, and various wood products. Some of it was produced locally, but, by this time, much of it was imported. In 1850, Blethen and his crew produced vessels valued at $8400. Blethen's yard was about half the size of the nearby Rufus Soule yard which was run by his wife's father and brother.

Shipbuilding at Porters Landing and elsewhere along the Maine coast was a complex operation. The design for a vessel was executed by a master builder, like Blethen, in the form of a half model. From the model, the lines of the vessel were laid out with chalk or pencil on the floor of the shipyard loft. Then templates or patterns could be made using thin boards.

The vessel itself was built on a gently sloping piece of ground, reinforced with timbers imbedded in the earth. First, the keel, or backbone, of the vessel was constructed of large timbers laid on a cribwork of blocks. Then other vertical timbers were added to form the frame of the ship. These had to be carefully shaped by hand so that the outside planking would fit correctly. The sawmill at Mast Landing may have cut rough timbers and planks for local builders like John Blethen. Planking was the next step. Steam was used to make the planks pliable so that they could be bent to fit the hull. Then caulkers sealed the seams with oakum and tar. At the same time, work was being done on the deck above. The rudder was hung and finally the finish carpentry—cabins, deck houses, railings, etc.—was completed. The full rigging might be done before or after the vessel was launched.

Most shipbuilders relied on other local craftsmen for certain parts of the vessel. Sails were made by expert sailmakers. Shipyards either had their own blacksmith or employed a local blacksmith to construct the needed metal parts. An 1851 map shows a blacksmith shop at Porters Landing. Rope was usually purchased. To decorate the bow, most vessels had a figurehead carved by a neighborhood artisan.

Ships' launchings were important community events, signifying the culmination of many months of labor. At Porters Landing, the launching of a vessel undoubtedly happened at high tide when there was nine feet, or more, of water.

After launching, the vessel was ready to carry the natural resources of New England throughout the world and return with goods from foreign ports.

half-hull

On Your Own at Porters Landing

Porters Landing: Most of the features of Porters Landing can be seen from South Street, which in the 1800s was the main route for goods coming through Porters Landing. Notice the house in which Shipwright John Blethen lived. It is the second house toward Freeport Village from the intersection of the Lower Mast Landing Road and South Freeport Road—on the same side of the road as Lower Mast Landing Road. The house was built before 1830 and was home to several families who had connections to the sea before John Blethen moved there in the mid-1800s.

This house has been greatly altered over the years. Originally it had a center chimney. Today, original period woodwork remains in only one room inside. There was a barn which burned in the 1960s.

Look at the other older houses in the area. Why do you suppose that those at Porters Landing are larger and more substantial than those at Mast Landing?

If you would like to stop for a minute, turn into the pull-out on the west side of South Street next to the pond. If the tide is low in the estuary, you will be able to see the extensive mud flats that are common along the Harraseeket. You will also notice a piece of modern technology, the Freeport Sewer District pumping station. There is a direct relationship between the health of the mud flats and the clams which live in them and the local sewage system. As the residents of Freeport switched from privies to flush toilets in the early 1900s, sewerage was dumped directly onto the mud flats, making the soft-shelled clams unsafe to eat. Pumping stations at Mast Landing and Porters Landing now move sewerage to a treatment plant on South Street, where it is treated before being emptied into the Harraseeket.

Clam Chowder: Cookbooks were a new phenomenon in the mid 1800s. Traditionally, recipes were handed down mother to daughter, or neighbor to neighbor. The following fish chowder recipe, or "receipt" as they were called then, is taken from *The Cook's Own Book* published in Boston in 1832. Mrs. Lee, the author, suggests that clam chowder *"May be made in the same way, substituting a sufficient quantity of clams instead of cod, the heads or hard leathery part being first cut off."* She goes on to say that many people *"prefer clam chowder, nicely cooked, to chowder made of cod, haddock, etc."*

Chowder For Ten Or Twelve

Take of salt pork cut in thin slices, as much as will make half a pint of fat, when tried, which will do for two good sized cod or haddock. Be careful not to burn the fat. First, put your fat in the pot. Secondly, cut your fish in as large pieces as will go into the pot; then put a layer of fish on the fat; pepper, salt and a few cloves, then a layer of the slices of pork, strewed over with onions cut fine; then a layer of shipbread or hard crackers dipped in water; then your thickening. Go on again with fish, & c. & c. as above, till your pot is nearly full, then put in water until you can just see it, and let it stew slowly, so as not to break the fish. After coming to a boil, it will be done in twenty-five or thirty minutes. N.B.—Some like potatoes cut in slices, which may be introduced between each layer. Likewise wine or cider, as you fancy. . . .

clamdigging

4 South Freeport

brace - ca. 1850

South from Porters Landing lies the village of South Freeport where there were four major shipyards in the latter 1800s. The Soule Brothers yard was the largest and most active. Vessels were launched from this yard for forty years from 1839 until 1879. Local wood, and wood brought from as far away as Canada, was used to build vessels that linked Freeport with the markets of the world.

The days of wooden sailing ships ended with the coming of steam-powered vessels, and most shipbuilding activity on the Harraseeket came to a halt at that time. Main Street of South Freeport still has the look of a prosperous nineteenth-century village, but some of the props are missing—the giant wooden schooners, barks, and brigs, themselves; the ways jutting out into deep water; the sounds of hammers and mallets; and the voices of the men in the yards. One can feel their presence, though, in the orderly procession of houses lining the street and in the seabreeze blowing against one's face.

South Freeport was known as Strout's Point Village, or simply "the Point," until the 1850s. The establishment of a post office in 1854 probably initiated the use of the term South Freeport to distinguish the area from the part of town served by the main post office in Freeport Village.

Today's residents look out onto the estuary of the Harraseeket as did their predecessors 100 years ago. Through the small opening between Stockbridge Point and the tip of Wolf Neck, the seawater of Casco Bay rushes in twice each day with the tide. With the tides move many of the members of the water community, feeding, and, in turn, being fed upon by larger predators. The smallest of the organisms are microscopic plants and animals which grow by the billions. These animals are food for various fish which also move between the estuary and Casco Bay. The number of larger species in the estuary is dependent on the available amount of microscopic plants and animals. Food supply is greatest in the spring and early summer. Therefore, this is the time that the largest numbers of fish and shellfish are found in the estuary.

Many species of fish are not permanent residents, but visit the estuary at certain times of the year to feed or spawn. For instance, from May through October, bluefish and pogies feed in the estuary. In the spring alewives can be found there. Tommycod or frostfish, a favorite of Mainers, travel up the estuary as far as Mast Landing Sanctuary to spawn in early winter. Mummichogs can be seen year-round in the Harraseeket and are often caught and used live as fishing bait. At various times, brook trout and striped bass are present in the estuary, and mackerel will come to the outer reaches of the Harraseeket. There is also a small scallop bed. One can readily see that the estuary provides a rich feeding and spawning ground for a variety of fish species.

Of course, the fish in turn provide food for other fish, birds, and mammals. Seals, which feed on alewives and pogies, often follow them into the estuary. Another marine mammal, the sea mink, was possibly a resident of the Harraseeket during the early 1800s. The animal was larger than its inland relative, with a coarser fur, and, while it is now extinct, skeletal remains have been found in Casco Bay. Manly Hardy, who had reportedly traded 50,000 mink skins with Penobscot Indians, wrote in a 1903 issue of *Forest and Stream* that the sea mink became extinct about 1860, or somewhat later.*

As one resident pointed out in a letter to the *Maine Farmer*, the leading agricultural publication in Maine in the 1800s, shipbuilding and shipping were the major economic activities at South Freeport in the middle of the last century. C. Pearl also relates in his letter of June 11, 1863, that some *"men and boys"* profited from the fisheries of the area.

The industries of this region are largely devoted to ship building and navigation. But there is also an active group in the clam digging and preparation of fish bait. Several hundred barrels of shelled clams are put up at our wharves for the cod and macherel fisheries, giving exciting and profitable employment to men and boys.

Later in the century, in 1886, a fish packing plant was opened to capitalize on the productive fisheries of the area. Cod, clams, and crabs were packed, or canned in South Freeport into this century. Lobster fishing and clamming still provide *"exciting and profitable employment"* to men and boys of Freeport.

*Cited in Alfred J. Godin, Wild Mammals of New England. *Baltimore: John Hopkins University Press, 1977*

Members of the South Freeport Community - 1860 Freeport, Maine

Heads of Households (Number of Occupants)

Clergymen
Amory Tyler (6)
Shipmasters
Isaac Pinkham (8)
Clement Soule (6)
Enos Soule (9)
Frank Soule (5)
Ambrose Talbot, Jr. (5)
Enoch Talbot (8)
Ladies
Sarah Kelsey (4)
Merchants
Gersham Bliss (5)
Master Carpenters
Horace Brewer (3)
Ship Carvers
Emery Jones (5)
Blacksmiths
Simon P. Higgins (4)
Patrick McConley (3)
Sailmakers
Charles Paine (3)
Albert Waite (8)
Joshua Waite, Jr. (2)
Otis Winslow (3)
Ship Carpenters
Amos Allen (9)
Emery Brewer (7)
James Brewer, Jr. (4)
William Chase (2)
William E. Chase (5)
Robert B. Dunham (4)
Gershom Lincoln (5)
Charles Pratt (4)

Benjamin P. Soule (5)
Joshua C. Soule (5)
Edmund A. Ward (3)
Ship Joiners
William H. Dunham (2)
House and Ship Joiners
Ambrose Curtis (7)
Edward P. Merrill (5)
L. M. Randall (4)
Joiners
Elijah S. Allen (4)
Anderson Litchfield (4)
Elias Wilson (3)
Spar Makers
Benjamin Chadsey (6)
William H. Chadsey (4)
Robert M. Dunham (3)
Caulkers
William Morse (3)
William H. Townsend (3)
House Joiners
Ambrose Osgood (7)
Carpenters
George Corliss (6)
Stevedores
Benjamin Dennison (6)
Mariners
William Bucknam (4)
Oliver Corliss (4)
J. McHenry Johnson (8)
Albert Rogers (4)
Fishermen
Alfred Bartol (6)
John Fonahue (2)

William Johnson (5)
Edward Payson (6)
William H. Randall (3)
Farmers
Barnaby Carver (4)
John W. Pratt (7)
J. Stockbridge (7)
Bailey Talbot (5)
Floyd Talbot (3)
Joshua Waite (2)
Farm Laborers
Ammi Mitchell (4)
Samuel Moore (4)
Daniel Talbot (8)
Dressmakers
Sarah Bliss (3)
No Listed Occupation
Margaret Abbot (1)
Jane Chase (4)
George Coffin (4)
Mariah Stockbridge (1)

Abundance of Community Members

```
                                    Low                                          High
Schoolchildren (male/female)        ─────────────────────────────────────────────80
Wives (female)                      ─────────────────────────────────59
Ship Carpenters (male)              ─────────────13
Mariners (male)                     ───────────11
Shipmasters (male)                  ─────────9
Fisherman (male)                    ─────────9
Farmers (male)                      ─────────9
Spar Makers (male)                  ─────4
House and Ship Joiners (male)       ───3
Joiners (male)                      ───3
Merchants (male)                    ───3
Carpenters (male)                   ───3
Sailmakers (male)                   ───3
Caulkers (male)                     ──2
Farm Laborers (male)                ──2
Servants (female)                   ──2
Blacksmiths (male)                  ──2
Ship Carvers (male)                 1
Ship Joiners (male)                 1
Stevedores (male)                   1
House Joiners (male)                1
Congregational Clergymen (male)     1
Dressmakers (female)                1
Ladies (female)                     1
Factory Operators (female)          1
Housekeepers (female)               1
Coasters (male)                     1
Students ("19 years old")           1
```

NOTE: Includes people believed to have lived at South Freeport in 1860 based on contemporary maps and deeds and the United States Census. The 1860 Census does not differentiate between the socio-economic communities of the Harraseeket District nor include "wife" as a category reported. "Schoolchildren" indicates people who have attended school within the year.

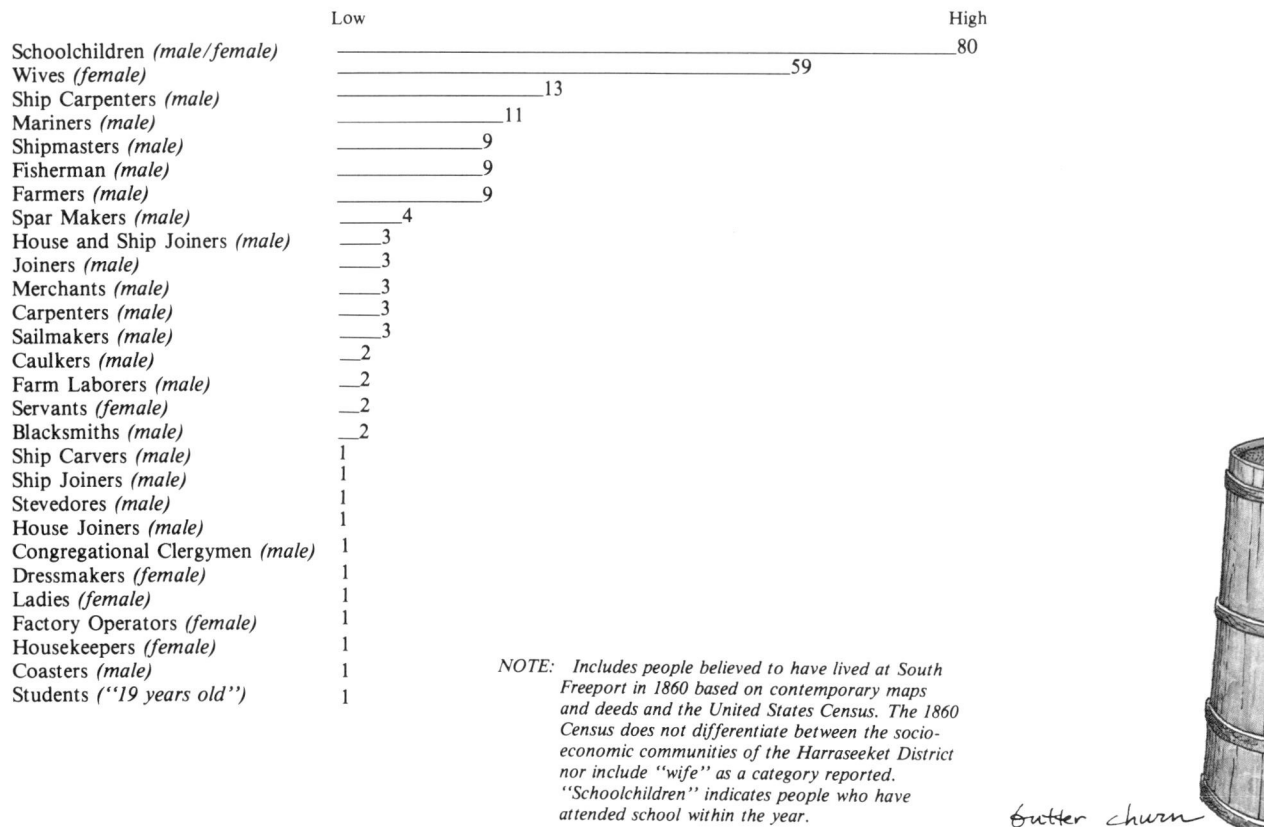

butter churn

52

Members of the Estuarine Water Community — 1980s Maine
Taxonomic Group (Number of Species)*

Animal Kingdom

Chordates:

Mammals
humans (1)
porpoises (1)
deer (1)
muskrats (1)
seals (1)
otters (1)
raccoons (1)

Birds
ospreys (1)
eagles (1)
kingfishers (1)
gulls & terns (10)
geese & ducks (21)
cormorants (2)
grebes (3)
loons (2)

Fishes
sticklebacks (4)
killifishes (2)
lampreys (1)
spiny dogfishes (1)
skates (3)
herrings (4)
trout & salmon (4)
smelts (1)
eels (1)
pipefishes (1)

codfishes (6)
redfishes (1)
sea basses (2)
bluefish (1)
sand lances (1)
mackerel (1)
pricklebacks (1)
cunners (1)
rock gunnels (1)
eelpouts (1)
silversides (1)
sea ravens (1)
sculpins (3)
alligator fishes (1)
wrymouths (1)
snailfishes (1)
lumpfishes (1)
flounders (5)
goosefishes (1)

Arthropods:

Insects (+)

Spiders & Mites (25+)

Crustaceans
shrimps (+)
copepods (11)
amphipods (+)
isopods (+)

Molluscs:

Bivalves (1)

Rotifers (+)

Segmented Worms (+)

Roundworms (+)

Ribbonworms (+)

Flatworms (+)

Comb Jellies (2)

Collenterates:

Jellyfish (2+)

Plant Kingdom

Diatoms (+)

Dinoflagellates (+)

Protista Kingdom

  Ciliates (+)

  Foraminifera (+)

  Radiolarians (+)

  Flagellates (+)

Monera Kingdom

  Blue-green Algae (+)

  Bacteria (+)

Abundance of Community Members

Community Member	Low → High
Diatoms	——————————————*
Dinoflagellates	——————————————*
Rotifers	——————————————*
Molluscs	——————————————*
Arthropods	——————————————*
Flagellates	—————————*
Ciliates	—————————*
Bacteria	———*
Blue-green Algae	———*
Radiolarians	———*
Foraminifera	———*
Collenterates	———*
Comb Jellies	———*
Flatworms	———*
Ribbonworms	———*
Roundworms	———*
Segmented Worms	———*
Chordates	*

Atlantic salmon

* "(+)" indicates number of species unknown/numerous.

NOTE: Includes adult organisms that commonly float, swim, or dive in the open water and channels of estuaries. Species selection based on personal observation; Ecological Characterization of Coastal Maine *(Newton Corner, MA: U.S. Fish and Wildlife Service, October, 1980);* and consultation with biologists. Many coastal Maine species are not represented in the four biotic communities chosen for the text.

Profile: Susan and Louisa Talbot

Women of the 1800s were very involved in processing natural products for market or family use. The diaries of Susan and Louisa Talbot, unmarried sisters who lived with their parents in South Freeport, detailed the numerous and varied activities of local farm women in their diaries. A significant part of their time was spent preparing cloth, clothing, and bedding for the family. Garments had to be washed and ironed, and before the washing could be done, Susan, Louisa, their sister and their mother had to make the soap, using fat from slaughtered animals. On one occasion, Susan reported, *"Mother finished making soap—I thought she would trot her legs off before she got through but she hasn't quite."* Candles also were made from animal tallow. Mattresses were sewn and then filled with corn husks gathered from the fields.

Food preparation took a large percentage of the women's time. As there were few processed foods, all food preparation, with the exception of grain milling, was done on the homestead itself. Susan and Louisa mentioned gathering berries for pies and jams, making both skim and hogshead cheese, filling sausages, frying fat to render lard, "picking" chickens, cleaning tripe and pigs feet, smoking hams, churning butter and tending gardens. Further activity was necessary to actually put food on the table. Baking apple, strawberry, blueberry, rhubarb, and pumpkin pies was frequently mentioned by Susan and Louisa. One day in January of 1867, *"mother baked 14 pies which I [Susan] filled & sweetened and cut the apples for."* Added to the baking was the preparation of main

nineteenth-century kitchen implements

dishes like beans and chowders.

Of course, women were also responsible for general housecleaning, indoor maintenance such as painting and papering, and child care. Although the men often grew and gathered natural products, the women had an equally important role in processing these products to make them useful to people.

Profile: Mackerel

The mackerel is one of many finfish found in the Harraseeket estuary and is probably the most common fish in the Gulf of Maine. The commercial use of mackerel has varied throughout the 1800s and 1900s. Before 1815, relatively few mackerel were harvested from the Gulf of Maine. After that date, the numbers of mackerel in the market increased. For local markets, mackerel was sold fresh, but for distant locations like the West Indies, it was pickled in a salt solution. After 1850, the demand for mackerel increased until about 1900 when demand and production declined.

Today, although mackerel are harvested by seiners along the Maine coast, they do not enjoy the popularity of fish such as herring. The outer reaches of the Harraseeket estuary have been the summer home of small schools of mackerel in recent years. They are fished by sport fishermen for home consumption.

The mackerel is a long, sleek, streamlined fish adapted for speed and maneuverability in open waters. Its body is various shades of blue and green on the sides, and silvery-white below. It has dark stripes on its back. "Mackerel" clouds were named because they resemble these back markings.

mackerel

Mackerel travel in schools and are superbly adapted to life in the watery world of the Gulf of Maine. An air bladder allows mackerel and other fish to remain at any level in the water without the effort of swimming. Their streamlined shape, rigid skeleton and powerful muscles all help mackerel move quickly to avoid the many other fish that would make a meal of them. The fins provide balance, steering, and braking. The fish get their oxygen by drawing water over their gills where the blood near the surface of the gill exchanges waste gasses for oxygen in the water. Like all bony fish, mackerel possess all of the traditional senses of sight, touch, smell, taste, and hearing, plus a sixth sense which is not fully understood, but is apparently associated with the detection of vibrations in the water.

Along the coast of Maine, mackerel usually appear in late spring and disappear in autumn. In some summers there has been an abundance of these fish, while in other years their numbers have been much fewer. The movements of mackerel schools are unpredictable because the fish follow food supplies and urgings of the spawning instinct. Their food includes small fish larvae, smaller adult fish, and shrimp. In spite of their power and speed, the mackerel themselves are fed upon by still larger fish like tuna, bluefish, cod, and dogfish, and by mammals such as whales and seals. They are one of the many species that form the complex pattern of life in estuaries like the Harraseeket.

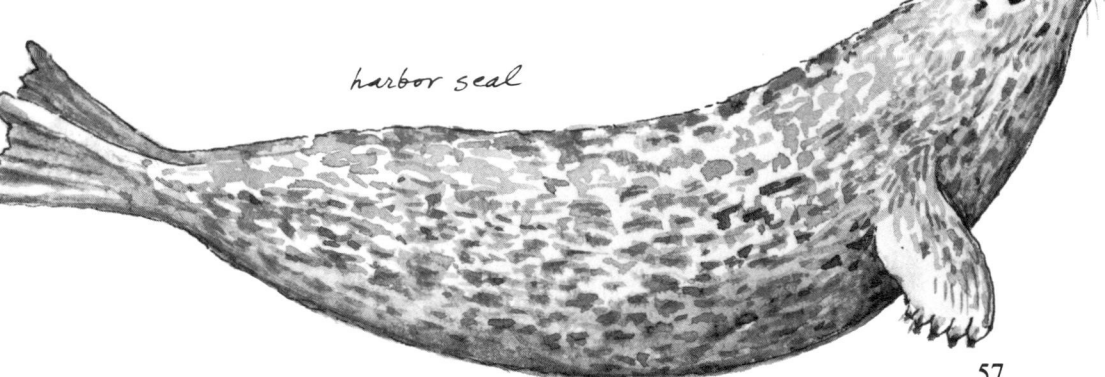
harbor seal

San Joaquin, 1876

On Your Own In South Freeport

Town Landing: Drive down Main Street and park at the Town Landing. From here you can see the location of all of the South Freeport shipyards. Shipyards were not fancy affairs in the 1800s. The ships were constructed out in the open, right along the shore, with their bows nudged up to the embankment. There is much more flat land here now than there was in the 1800s. The granite ways where ships were launched, pilings from wharves, and a large area of mud flat are now buried under many feet of landfill dumped here in the 1970s. Look closely at the building on your left as you face the harbor (east). It was probably built as a warehouse by the Strouts Point Wharf Company, an organization of local men whose purpose was to build *"such wharfs and stores as may be found necessary in the Town of Freeport."* What kind of a foundation does the building have? Why?

Look up the Harraseeket to the north and you will see the site of the Cushing and Briggs shipyard projecting out into the estuary from the west side. At the height of shipbuilding activity in the 1850s, two other small shipyards were also located along the edge of the Harraseeket between the Soule yard at the Town Landing and Cushing-Briggs to the north.

The land to the east, across the

schooner

great blue heron

Harraseeket, is Wolf Neck. The enormous white barn directly across the estuary was built as part of Edmund B. Mallet's farming operation.

Look south, out through the mouth of the Harraseeket into Casco Bay. The incoming tide rushes through this opening twice each day, bringing with it several varieties of fish, some feeding on microscopic plants and animals, and others feeding on smaller fish. Birds like cormorants and great blue herons can usually be seen hunting for food in the area.

The Great Blue Heron is a well known bird along the estuary. The majestic flight of the Great Blue, with its broad wings flapping in slow motion, its neck curled, and its legs trailing behind, is a common sight over the Harraseeket. At other times these birds can be seen standing motionless in shallow water, waiting for an unsuspecting fish to swim by.

steamer   hampton boat   gundalow   dory

Boat Watching: Hundreds of boats are moored in the lower Harraseeket during the summer. Only a handful are fishing vessels which unload lobsters and other catch on the wharf. The vast bulk of the boats—about 500— are pleasure craft indicating the increased amount of capital and leisure time residents of the Freeport area have accumulated since the town was first settled in the 1700s. Although most of the boats are used for recreation, their design evolved from working sailing vessels of the 1700s and 1800s. In the 1800s, the illustrated types of boats were probably common on the Harraseeket. How many of them can you spot today?

ship   bark   brig   Schooner

Ferry To Bustins Island: During the summer months a private company offers a passenger ferry service to Bustins Island. Check at the nearby restaurant for current fees and schedules. The Island is a summer colony that has not changed much since it was established in the early 1900s. There are no public services or public areas on the island, so stay on board the ferry and take the return trip to the Harraseeket. The stone tower of Casco Castle, a summer hotel built at the beginning of this century, can be seen on the hill above the South Freeport waterfront. The ferry is a pleasurable way to see the estuary from a boat, which is the same perspective from which many residents saw the estuary during the 1800s.

Main Street: Watch for two prominent styles of houses, Federal and Greek Revival, as you retrace your route up Main Street. Federal style houses were built after the American Revolution. In Freeport they tend to be one-and-a-half story, low-roofed structures, with windows arranged symmetrically around a central doorway, often topped with an elaborate fanlight or window.

The Greek Revival style enjoyed a long period of popularity, from the 1840s to the Civil War. This style imitates the classical designs of ancient Greece, and the more elaborate houses look like temples with columns and pediments. The Greek Revival influence can be seen

Federal style

in the trim of even modest homes. Why do you suppose the new Federal style appeared after the Revolution, and why would Americans want to imitate classic Greek temples?

As you travel back up Main Street away from the shore, you will see two houses at the top of the rise. The one on the left, a large two-and-a-half story structure, towers above the street. The story-and-a-half house on the right rests more gently on the land. Both homes have commanding views of the Harraseeket estuary and the waterfront, just what the shipyard owners who lived there would have wanted.

Enos Soule built the taller home. He and two of his brothers, Clement and Henchman, started the Soule Brothers shipyard here, completing their first ship in 1839. Altogether the company launched about 30 vessels before it closed in 1879. Constructed around 1852, this house is a plain, rather large example of the Greek Revival style. Most of the homes in the South Freeport village are Greek Revival, indicating that most of the construction occurred during the busy and prosperous days of the shipyards.

The smaller house is of the earlier architectural style — the Federal style. It was built between 1831 and 1834 by Alfred Soule, a ship captain, and bought by Samuel Bliss in 1846. Shortly afterwards,

Greek Revival style

Charles and Gershom Bliss started the Bliss Brothers yard on the shore in front of the house. The company built mostly small fishing schooners, but also constructed several larger vessels. This house looks quite different from the Enos Soule homestead across the street. The trim is much more delicate and the windows have smaller panes. There is an elliptical opening over the door where a fanlight was once located, and below it are sidelights with a lacy pattern of glass. There are several houses like this along Main Street, showing the taste of the people who lived here before the big shipyards opened.

If you travel further up Main Street to the intersection with Harraseeket Road, you can see, on the right, the building which used to be the post office and store for the village. Although it has since been turned into apartments, it still has the look of a commercial building.

Built between 1853 and 1857 by Samuel Osgood, it was operated as a store until the 1960s and as a post office until 1972.

Continuing up Main Street, notice the cottage on the left side just beyond the store. It was built around 1890 when Maine began to be a haven for "summer folk" and is representative of the "Stick Style" architecture. While only a few summer cottages were built in the village itself, several groups of cottages were constructed along the shore to the east, and out on Bustins Island. The other homes on both sides of the street are typical of those constructed during the shipbuilding boom. One-and-a-half stories tall, they have simple Greek Revival trim. A favorite motif was the doorway framed by wide pilasters and full length sidelights.

Keep going to the intersection where Middle Street joins Main Street from the left. This is a good place to admire one of the most elaborate homes in the village, which is set back on the right side of the street. Two of the three bays of its facade are recessed behind tall columns, giving it a majestic appearance. It is thought that George W. Randall, a local house and ship joiner, designed this house. He chose elements of the Italianate style—brackets and a bay window—as well as of the Greek Revival style to adorn this building. It was built for Ambrose Curtis, also a ship joiner.

From here, too, you can see that most of the houses have barns. While the village was, indeed, more urban than the surrounding countryside back in the 1800s, families provided a lot of their own food. The barns probably sheltered a milk cow, pigs and hens, and perhaps a horse and carriage. Old maps and photographs show that much of what we see as woods today

used to be hay fields, pastures, and garden plots.

Winslow Park: Turn left onto South Freeport Road at the crossroads. You will pass by the post office, store, church, and school that mark the modern social center of South Freeport. One half mile from the crossroads you will pass the Talbot farm on your left. It was here that Susan and Louisa Talbot spent most of their days during the latter half of the 1800s, and an entry from Louisa's diary illustrates the inescapable contact that people of the past had with the natural environment. On January 17, 1867, she wrote *"A cold blustering snow storm, the wind hurls the snow in eddies and into every nook and crannle [of the house]. I never saw anything like it, in this house or any other."* One mile from the crossroads is Staples Point Road. Follow it to Winslow Park.

Winslow Park is maintained by the Town of Freeport. From Memorial Day through Labor Day it is operated as a camping area, mostly for recreational vehicles. There is also a popular public swimming beach which is usable at high tide. A small fee is charged for day use of the park. The best time to visit the Park is during the off-season. Park in the pull-off by the entrance gate being sure that you don't block access to the boat ramp. Follow the service road and perimeter trail along the northern shore to the tip of Stockbridge Point. There are several private residences on the point, so please respect the owners' privacy. From here you have a full view of the lower Harraseeket, flanked by South Freeport village on the left and Wolf Neck on the right. Depending on the tide, the surface water is either flowing in or out of the mouth of the Harraseeket, rushing by Pumpkin Knob and Pound of Tea, the two islands that mark the end of the Harraseeket estuary and the beginning of Casco Bay.

Retrace your path back to the parking area. Along the way, notice the farmhouse that sits in the middle of the camping area. The main part of the house may have been built by John Cushing or his son in the 1790s. In his diary, Cushing mentioned that both he and his son built houses on this point of land. Until he moved into Freeport Village in 1793, Cushing grew wheat, barley, peas, potatoes, corn, beans, oats, cabbage, turnips, salt hay, and flax for linen on this farm. The land was used for agriculture from approximately 1750 to 1900. Oxen, cows, sheep, and pigs were also raised. Nearby, the Cushings produced bricks in their brickyard.

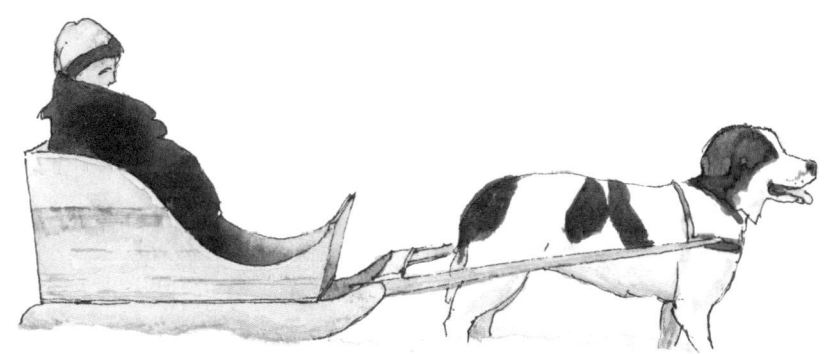

Part III - Conclusion

So. Freeport, 1983

What changes have occurred in the landscape and within the communities of the Harraseeket district since the 1800s? The land has changed very little. Some of the easily eroded clay soil covering the bedrock of the Harraseeket watershed has been washed into the estuary by rainwater and melting snows, resulting in many narrow, finger-like gullies along the shore. The channel of the estuary has been shaped and reshaped by the flow of the tide as it moves the added clay material back and forth, forming new mud flats and eating away at the banks of the Harraseeket. The water itself has undergone minor changes in temperature, generally warming, and in chemical makeup. The tides have gradually been bringing the water of the estuary farther up onto the shore, the result of world-wide adjustments between continents and sea level that followed the last ice age. For the last 4,000 years the water has risen in relation to the land about 1/10 inch per year. On the Harraseeket, this means that today's average high tide rises about one foot higher on the shore than the average high tide in 1869, when the *Daniel L. Choate* was launched at Porters Landing. These changes may be significant to an individual plant or animal affected by shifting mud and changing water temperature, or to someone owning a building near the shore. But when compared to the changes that shaped the Harraseeket watershed over the millenia of geologic time, the land and water have remained relatively the same since the the 1800s. New buildings have been added to the landscape since the last century, of course, but they have, for the most part, been built in between the buildings that stood when Samuel Banks, Joel Kelsey, John Blethen, Susan and Louisa Talbot, and their contemporaries lived along the shores of the Harraseeket. The backdrop of life in the Harraseeket district today is much as it was in the 1800s.

The communities living in the landscape have changed considerably since the last century, particularly the socio-economic communities. While a social identity, a sense of "community" or neighborhood, still exists in the settlements of the Harraseeket district, the economic identity of the communities there has all but vanished. Few people living on Wolf Neck continue to earn their livelihood from farming as residents did a century ago. In the later 1800s industry and commerce moved away from the settlements of Mast Landing, Porters Landing, and South Freeport and became concentrated in Freeport Village where there were better highway and railroad connections. The turn of the century, from the 1800s to the 1900s, was a time of transition in the socio-economic communities of the Harraseeket district—a transition that was tied to the economic growth of Freeport Village.

Freeport Village got its start as an intersection of two roads in the interior of Freeport. The early name of the area indicates the impact that those roads, and land transportation in general, have had on the growth of the village. At first, the area was called Freeport Corner, or simply "the Corner," which contrasts with the terms "landing," "neck," and "point," which were all parts of the early names of the four Freeport settlements on the shores of the Harraseeket. In the late 1700s, the Jameson Tavern, now a restaurant on Main Street, was a way station for the stage coaches that traveled the rough coastal road through Freeport. Travel by water was without a doubt the easiest form of transportation, but roads became necessary for travel to inland areas, for transporting goods during the winter, and to drive cattle to market. In 1849, the railroad came to Freeport Village and, with it, the ability to transport goods economically over long distances. Flour ground from mid-western wheat became readily available in the Freeport area, and manufactured products from Freeport's new industries could easily be shipped to distant inland markets. In 1890, the Maine Central Railroad reports that 15,035 passengers left the Freeport railroad station on Depot Street.

The steam engine was the driving force behind changes in transportation in the last half of the 1800s, as well as changes in people's lifestyles. The first trains were pulled into Freeport Village by steam-powered locomotives and, at the same time, steam-powered, propeller-driven craft appeared on the Harraseeket. By the late 1800s, regularly scheduled steamboat service connected Freeport with Portland and other ports on Casco Bay, offering two trips daily in summer. Eventually, steamboats replaced sailing vessels as the major means of transportation worldwide, and iron hulls replaced wooden ones. The drastic decline in demand for wooden sailing ships closed the shipyards on the shores of the Harraseeket (although the Soule yard was opened again between 1914 and 1918 to build wooden vessels for the United States Navy during World War I). While the shipyards were closing, new steam-powered factories were being built in Freeport Village. The steam engine powered the Industrial Revolution both here and in Europe. Its major advantages were that it could be placed almost anywhere unlike the old mills which required falling water, and operators could change its speed or direction at will. It could easily be adapted to drive pumping plants, air compressors, and shafts for machine shops, rolling mills and saw mills. In Freeport, the use of steam power rejuvenated a sagging economy and began to shape "modern" lifestyles.

The careers of Captain Rufus Soule Randall and Edmund B. Mallet, Jr., both prominent residents of the Village in the 1880s, illustrate the changes that were taking place in peoples' lives at the turn of the century. Captain Randall began his seagoing career in 1841 when, at the age of 11, he signed on as a general cook and "roustabout" boy on the

steam and sail

packet *Nathan Nye* which ran from Porters Landing to Portland. In the years that followed, Randall sailed to many ports around the world marketing the natural products of New England, such as ice and lumber. At least two of his vessels, the *Oasis* and the *John A. Briggs*, were built in Freeport yards. It is evident in the following quote from his diaries, written soon after he left port in 1865, that both the land and sea held their charms for Randall.

> *Blue water & plenty of gulfweed—I like the 'Acadia' so far verry well—wish I owned a piece of her to sail in for a spell. What a change in mode of life this is for me after being farming for the last ye [year] & 6 months. Old ocean! with all thy treachery I love thee still—. . .*
>
> *But I shall* in a few years to retire on a good farm (*wish to).*

In 1877, Randall purchased a house lot in Freeport Village and, following a pattern typical of many sea captains of his time, retired to farm life with his wife and eight children (several of whom were born in foreign ports on board ship). Until his death in 1886, Randall divided his time between tending his farm animals and orchard, and going to sea.

Edmund B. Mallet, the most prominent of Freeport's industrialists, began his career in the village as Captain Randall was retiring to his farm. Mallet invested a large inheritance in a variety of steam-powered industries, including shoe factories, a saw mill, and a grist mill. He also operated a coal yard, brickyard, lumberyard, and several granite quarries and he owned a large department store, employing twelve clerks, which carried dry goods, groceries, hardware, and clothing. Mallet used his own products to build housing for the workers he employed. The *Industrial Journal*, a Bangor newspaper of the day, credited E. B. Mallet with single-handedly halting the decline of Freeport and providing for its prosperity.

Other people, following Mallet's lead, also started new businesses. An 1894 map of Freeport Village shows that it had three shoe and boot factories, a laundry, livery stables, a lumberyard, a printing shop, a photography studio, and a bakery. (One of the storeowners was a young man of 22 named Leon Leonwood Bean. In 1912, his new firm of L.L. Bean began catering to the latest trend in the use of natural resources—outdoor recreation.)

The differences in the lives of these two men—Captain Randall and E.B. Mallet—characterizes the differences between traditional ways of life and the emerging industrial lifestyle of Freeport at the turn of the century. Throughout most of the 1800s, peoples' everyday lives

included direct contact with the natural resources of the Harraseeket estuary and its surrounding land. Farmers, such as Samuel Banks, used the products of the land and water to provide food, clothing and shelter. The Talbot sisters were typical of women of the day in their role of making farm products useful for the rest of the family. Surpluses were sent to market in ships built and launched into the estuary by men like John Blethen. It was not uncommon for a man to be both a farmer and a seaman in his lifetime, and Captain Randall's choice of this traditional lifestyle put him in daily contact with the elements of wind, water, and soil, requiring a wide range of skills. E. B. Mallet, on the other hand, was part of a new breed of industrialists who chose to utilize a new mechanical source of power, the steam engine, to develop a factory-based economy dependent upon distant natural resources, drawing laborers out of farm fields and shipyards and into a life of single-skill wage labor in Freeport Village factories. Land transportation and factory work became the norm rather than the exception in Freeport by the end of the 1800s.

As the twentieth century began, the Portland and Brunswick Electric Street Railway and the automobile arrived in Freeport Village. The trolley was short-lived, but, of course, automobile use increased. U.S. Route One and Interstate-95 now carry thousands of tourists into Freeport each year. Almost half the working residents of Freeport leave by car each morning for jobs in other towns. Half of the residents employed in Freeport work in manufacturing. Daily physical contact with the soil, wood, water, clams, or salt hay of the Harraseeket watershed is the pursuit of few of its modern residents. People have forfeited intimate contact with their local environment and clocks, rather than tides and seasons, now regulate their lives.

Red Pine cone

In addition to these profound changes in the socio-economic communities, the biotic communities of the Harraseeket district have also changed since the 1800s. The upland community had been laboriously cleared of trees early on, as Reverend Nason reported, but today many of the fields of the 1800s have returned to woodlands.

Some local pine and spruce are harvested for pulpwood and sawlogs, and hardwoods are cut for firewood. Freeport oak is used to build lobster traps and, along with other kinds of local wood, it is used for some boat repair. But the days of shipbuilding from local wood are over. Diseases imported from Europe have reduced the vigor of white pines, killed mature chestnuts, and all but eliminated elm trees from the upland community.

There have been other additions and losses. The Starling was brought from Europe, released near New York City, and has since become common in Freeport. Likewise, the Japanese Beetle, first discovered on plants in New Jersey in 1916, is now common here. The Timber Wolf, Woodland Caribou, and Elk are among the animals which, like chestnut trees, were once common in coastal Maine but no longer can be found.

The salt marshes of the Harraseeket escaped the indiscriminate filling and alteration that occurred elsewhere during the 1800s and 1900s. In the 1970s, government took action to control the uses of marshland, and legislation currently helps protect the marshes and mud flats of the Harraseeket estuary. Today, people limit their use of the marshes to the hunting of deer and waterfowl. Recently a small number of trappers, from Freeport and elsewhere, have come to the marshes for the muskrat, fisher, mink, raccoon, fox, and beaver furs. Salt hay hasn't been harvested for fifty years.

The most dramatic change in the mud flat community since the 1800s has been the rise in the number of harmful bacteria caused by dumping inadequately treated sewage into the Harraseeket. Since the opening of the sewage treatment plant in 1977, and the passage of laws prohibiting the overboard discharge of human wastes from boats in the harbor, bacteria harmful to humans have decreased significantly. Flats once closed by pollution have been reopened for the harvesting of clams. The Town of Freeport issues licenses to up to 100 commercial clammers each year, who dig soft-shelled clams from the mud flats in a manner not unlike the Indian clammers of centuries before.

The water community supports from ten to twelve fulltime lobstermen who ply their trade from spring to winter freeze-up. Edible fish such as brook trout, striped bass, bluefish, mackerel, and smelt are caught in the estuary, though mostly for home consumption. The safe harbor of the Harraseeket sustains two marinas and related businesses. Boats that evolved from the work boats of the past are now used for recreation.

The water community has not changed drastically since the 1800s; most of the same animals (fish, shell fish, plankton, and birds) and plants still thrive in the waters of the Harraseeket. Two exceptions are the wild oyster, which is no longer common along the coast of Maine, and the snowy egret, which is a relative newcomer to the waters of the Harraseeket.

During this century, the steam-engine inspired lifestyles of the late 1900s were reinforced by new technologies; the internal combustion engine further revolutionized transportation, new communication devices moved information quickly, and eventually the rocket engine began to power the exploration of space. Unlike the residents of the 1800s, whose vision of the world was an outward view anchored in knowledge of local communities, residents in the 1900s now view the Harraseeket district from the perspective of outer space where the entire earth is seen as a tiny ball of blue in the vastness of space. Intimate knowledge of the land and sea is no longer necessary to earn a livelihood for the majority of people who live on the shores of the Harraseeket estuary.

In recent years the study of the complex connections between plants, animals, and their environment has shown how fragile the life support systems are on spaceship earth. The "man vs. nature" attitude of early settlers is slowly being replaced by a philosophy of "people as a part of nature." Once again it is crucial for people to have knowledge of their local environment; not in order to earn a livelihood, but to protect the health of the planet. We—people, mackerel, clams, marsh grass, white pine and all other life forms within the Harraseeket district—are dependent on each other in a complex system of life that stretches throughout the watershed and to every corner of the globe. Concern for the health of the Harraseeket system is dependent on a concern for the larger systems of land, water, and air that circle the globe supporting interdependent communities of plants and animals.

Bibliography

Field Guides - The following guidebooks will be useful while exploring the Harraseeket district.

Beard, Frank A., *200 Years of Maine Housing: A Guide for the Housewatcher*. 3rd. ed., rev. Augusta, ME: Maine Historic Preservation Commission, 1981.
   Photos of Maine houses showing common architectural styles.

Green, Sharon et al., "A Teachers Guide to Wolf Neck Woods State Park." Maine Department of Conservation, 1977.
   Three sections: One on the ecology of the park; the second suggesting environmental education activities for children; the third listing further references. NOTE: Only available at B.H. Bartol Library, Freeport.

dipper

Hallowell, Anne C. and Barbara G., *Fern Finder: A Guide to Native Ferns of Northeastern and Central North America*. CA: Nature Study Guild, 1981.
   A handy pocket guide to ferns of northeastern and central North America.

Johnson, Judith, *Heritage of Our Maine Wildflowers*. Rockland, ME: Courier of Maine Books, 1979.
   Interesting information about past and present plant uses. Out of print but available at libraries.

Katona, Stephen K., Rough, Valerie and Richardson, David T. *A Field Guide to the Whales and Seals of the Gulf of Maine and Eastern Canada*. New York: Charles Scribner's Sons, 1983, Third Edition.
   Black and white illustrations.

Miller, Dorcas S., *The Maine Coast: A Nature Lover's Guide*. Charlotte, NC: East Woods Press Books, 1979.
   Natural history, flora, fauna. Section on Freeport, including "mast" mythology.

Newcomb, Lawrence, *Newcomb's Wildflower Guide*. Boston: Little, Brown & Co., 1977.
   A standard guide to wildflowers.

Petrides, George A., *A Field Guide to Trees and Shrubs*. Boston: Houghton Mifflin Co., 1972.
   A standard guide to trees and shrubs found in Freeport.

Pierson, Elizabeth Cary and Jan Erik, *A Birder's Guide to the Coast of Maine*. Camden, ME: Downeast Books, 1981.
   Includes tips on birding along the shore on the coast of Maine as well as places to go birding (does not include Freeport).

Robbins, S., *Birds of North America*. New York: Golden Press, 1966.
   One of several good field guides to birds.

Sadlier, Ruth and Paul, *Short Walks Along the Maine Coast*. Chester, CT: Pequot Press, 1977.
   Includes a walk for Wolf Neck Woods State Park.

Waters, John F., *Exploring New England Shores: A Beachcomber's Handbook*. Lexington, MA: Stone Wall Press, 1974.
   Includes flora, fauna, tides, ecology, aquariums, etc.

Zim, Herbert S. and Donald F. Hoffmeister, *Mammals: A Guide to Familiar American Species*. Racine, WI: Golden Press, New York & Western Publishing Co., 1955.
   A handy pocket guide to common mammals.

B. H. Bartol Library - The Freeport Library is located on Main Street, one block south of the L.L. Bean retail salesroom. Here you will find all of the books listed in the following General References section; the specific information listed below about the Harraseeket district; as well as many other books relating to history and ecology. The library is open weekday afternoons and some mornings and evenings. The library staff is more than willing to help you follow up on a topic. Don't hesitate to ask for their help.

Lowe, Vicki; Rand, Sally; and Wengren, Mary Eliza, "Architectural Survey of Freeport, Maine."
Augusta, ME: Maine Historic Preservation Commission, 1976.
   A card file containing facts about all of the houses in Freeport that were built before 1920 and still standing in 1974. Very comprehensive.

Harraseeket Interpretive Project, "1850s Coastal Life." Freeport, ME: 1983.
   A collection of research to date about the Harraseeket district in the 1850s. Includes information on saltwater farming, coastal food ways, and estuarine ecology.

Vertical File - detailed information about the Harraseeket district past and present. Ask the librarians for help.

General References - All of the following can be located at the B. H. Bartol Library in Freeport.

Apollonio, Spencer, *The Gulf of Maine*. Rockland, ME: Courier of Maine Books, 1979.
    An informative book about the geologic history, geography, and physical properties of the Gulf of Maine. Easy reading.

Chapelle, Howard I., *American Small Sailing Craft*. New York: W.W. Norton & Co., 1951.
    The classic reference on small craft. Photos.

Clancy, Edward P., *The Tides*. New York: Doubleday, Garden City, 1968.
    For those who really want to know how tides work. An understandable explanation of a technical subject.

Derevitsky, Catherine, *Lobsterpots and Searocket Sandwiches: A Guide to Edibles of the Seashore*. Merrill Marine by the author, 1979.
    Recipes for several of the plants and animals found in the Harraseeket. Good for all ages. Illustrated.

Dunn, William, *Casco Bay Steamboat Album*. Camden, ME: Downeast Enterprises, Inc., 1966.
    Photos and short descriptions of steamboats, including ones that plied the Harraseeket.

Farb, Jay, John and Porter, *The Atlantic Shore: Human and Natural History From Long Island to Labrador*. New York & Evanston: Harper & Row, 1969.
    A general reference as the title indicates but well worth reading. Easy style with excellent references.

Freeman, Bruce and Lionel Walford, *Anglers Guide to the U.S. Atlantic Coast. . .Passamaquoddy Bay, Maine, to Cape Cod*. National Oceanic and Atmospheric Administration, National Marine Fisheries Service, 1974.
    The best reference on marine fish. Good illustrations.

Godin, Alfred J., *Wild Mammals of New England*. Baltimore: John Hopkins University Press, 1977.
    Common mammals of New England, past and present. Interesting reading with several references to coastal Maine.

Greenhill, Basil, *Archaeology of the Boat: A New Introductory Study*. Middletown, CT: Weslcyan University Press, 1976.
    Includes boats built in New England. Illustrated with excellent bibliography.

Harvard University Fisher Museum of Forestry, *The Harvard Forest Models.* New York: Cornwall Press, 1975.

    Fascinating photos of models showing how the landscape of New England has changed since settlement.

Rowe, William H., *Ship Building Days on Casco Bay 1717-1890.* Freeport, ME: Bond Wheelwright Co., 1966.

    Boats built on the Harraseeket receive good coverage along with the people who built and sailed them. Mr. Rowe does not list any sources, however, so it is difficult to sort fact from hearsay. This work was drawn from research done for the *Maritime History of Maine.*

Russell, Howard S., *Long, Deep Furrow: Three Centuries of Farming in New England.* Hanover, NH: University Press of New England, 1982.

    A comprehensive history of New England agriculture with a chapter on saltwater farming. Good references. Illustrated.

Teal, John and Mildred, *Life and Death of the Salt Marsh.* New York: Ballentine Books, 1969.

    The best book available on the ecology of Atlantic salt marshes and estuaries, including how marshes developed and the life that inhabits them. Enjoyable reading. Highly recommended.

Thurston, Florence G. and Cross, Harmon S., *Three Centuries of Freeport, Maine.* Freeport: Bond Wheelwright, 1940.

    Filled with anecdotes and traditions about Freeport's past with, unfortunately, very little identification of sources. Successfully refutes the myth of Freeport as the "birthplace of Maine" in the only chapter with footnotes.

Ulrich, Laurel, *Good Wives: Images and Reality in the Lives of Women in Northern New England, 1650-1750.* New York: Knopf, 1982.

    One of the few books that describes the lives of early farm women. Text based on contemporary diaries.

Weitzman, David, *Underfoot: A Guide to Exploring and Preserving America's Past.* New York: Charles Scribner & Son, 1976.

    Enjoyable insights into the background of New England's cemeteries.

Zimiles, Martha and Murray, *Early American Mills.* New York: Crown Publishers, 1973.

    Good reference for both water-powered mills and steam-powered mills. Over 350 photos.

Acknowledgments

Text: Bruce Jacobson
Joel W. Eastman
Anne Bridges

Illustrations: Jon Luoma

Consultant: G. M. deLesseps

Design: M. Melissa Hatch

Thanks To:

The National Endowment for the Humanities for supporting the production of this document.

The Columbia Fund for funding staff.

The Maine Audubon Society for support services; for co-sponsoring the project; and for use of material from the *Report of the Commissioners of Fisheries and Game.*

The Freeport Historical Society for co-sponsoring the project; and for opening its archives to the authors.

Mrs. Margaret Bowden for use of material from the Susan and Louisa Talbot Diaries.

The Maine Historical Society for use of material from the *Dash* logbook, 1813-14; John Cushing Diary, typed copy, 1787-1811; Dillingham, John & Margaret, Papers, 1835-1857 Coll. 153; and for research assistance.

The Maine Maritime Museum for use of material from the Rufus Soule Randall Diaries 1860-1869, 1871-1877, 1881-1888; Rufus Soule Randall Daily Journal 1868-1869; and for research assistance.

The B. H. Bartol Library for research assistance.

The Fogler Library, University of Maine at Orono and its Special Collections for research assistance.

C. Raymond Thomas for use of material from the *S. Curtis Daybook, 1854;* and *The 1890 Report of the Maine Central Railroad.*

Verna Noble for use of a photo of Samuel Banks.

The following people for valuable information and for assisting with production: Jane Arbuckle, Betsy Bass, Liza Chandler, David Coffin, Jane Crozen, Bill Drury, David Emery, Gail Goldsmith, Becky Grant, Campbell Grant, Sarah Hartigan, Ed Hawes, Wes Hedlund, Carey Hotaling, Gary Hoyle, Steve Hyde, Dorothy Jacobson, George Jacobson, Steve Katona, Victor Konrad, Peter Larson, Kate LeRoyer, Mike Mazurkiewicz, Sara Kay McKenney-Hyatt, Marcell Moreau, Marilyn Norcini, Deb Pinham, Sally W. Rand, Ray Riciputi, Myra Siegel, Cheryl Smith, Winn Stowell, Elaine Tietjen, Pam Truesdale, Donna Vallas, Heidi Welch, and Mary Eliza Wengren.

Typeset at Lakeside Printing, Rockland, Maine

Printed at the Anthoensen Press, Portland, Maine

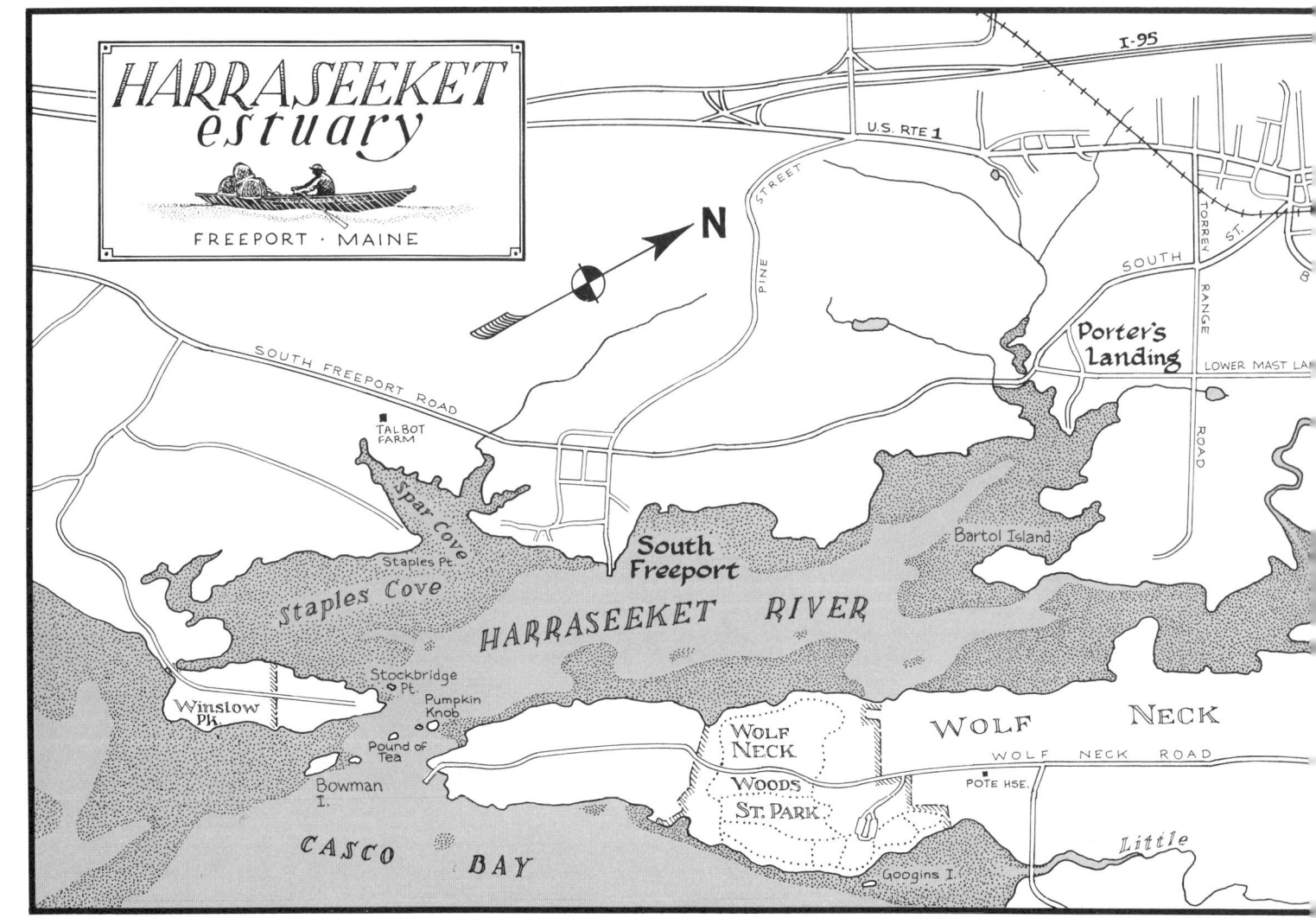